Twelfth Night

William Shakespeare

Guide written by John Mahoney

D1610655

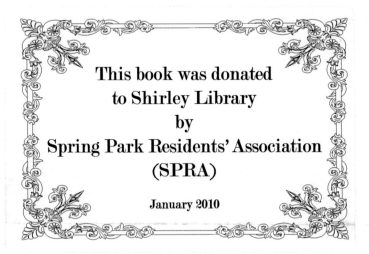

This book was donated
to Shirley Library
by
Spring Park Residents' Association
(SPRA)

January 2010

A *Letts* Literature Guide for GCSE

Contents

TWELFTH NIGHT

DUKE ORSINO IS LOVESICK FOR OLIVIA....

IF MUSIC BE THE FOOD OF LOVE, PLAY ON...

I'LL SERVE THIS DUKE.

VIOLA — CESARIO — HAS A MISSION

BE NOT DENIED ACCESS, STAND AT HER DOORS...

OLIVIA MOURNS FOR HER DEAD BROTHER.

I KNOW HIS SOUL IS IN HEAVEN

OLIVIA'S STEWARD DREAMS OF MARRYING HIS MISTRESS...

...AND SOME HAVE GREATNESS THRUST UPON 'EM.

MORE MATTER...

...FOR A MAY MORNING.

Viola

> ❝*She bore a mind that envy could not but but call fair*❞

This is Sebastian's assessment of his sister Viola, and it is perhaps the most accurate of all. We first meet Viola in Act 1 Sc 2. She has survived a shipwreck, but believes her brother may have died in the same catastrophe.

Viola determines to seek out the local governor, Orsino, and gain employment with him. Being a woman in a foreign land, she decides she will be safer if she disguises herself as a man. Then she lists her talents: 'I can sing / And speak to him in many sorts of music' (Act 1 Sc 2). Thus, she demonstrates practical thinking, swift decision-making and a business-like manner.

Because of her sensible approach, Viola is able to make judgements about situations and she is persistent and determined in the execution of her duties for the Duke. On her first visit to Olivia, she manages to talk her way into Olivia's presence. She is also loyal to the point of ignoring her own best interests. Even when she realises that she is in love with Orsino, she decides to carry on with her mission to win Olivia on Orsino's behalf.

As a woman she is also sensitive to her physical weakness. She is not happy at the thought of taking part in a duel, but nevertheless does not throw off her disguise: 'A little thing would make me tell them how much I lack of a man' (Act 3 Sc 4).'.

That Viola impresses others is clear. The Duke takes her into his confidence and admires her beauty: 'Diana's lip / Is not more smooth and rubious' (Act 1 Sc 4). Even the dour Malvolio calls her 'well-favoured', and Sir Andrew calls her 'a rare courtier'.

Olivia

A virtuous maid, the daughter of a count.

As the other major female character in the play, it is inevitable that we should contrast Olivia with Viola. To some extent their circumstances are the same. Both are well bred and come from well-to-do families. Both have recently suffered the loss of a brother. Yet their reactions to their losses are totally different. Olivia has decided to stay in mourning for seven years but she abandons her mourning as soon as a desirable young man, in the form of Cesario, arrives.

The Captain, a source of much information, describes her as 'fair Olivia' and a 'virtuous maid'. Orsino suggests that 'heaven walks on earth' when Olivia enters.

Viola has much opportunity to know Olivia, and gives this account of her: 'you are too proud: / But if you were the devil, you are fair' (Act 1 Sc 5). Sebastian, even on his short acquaintance with Olivia, makes a shrewd judgement about her capabilities. He tells how she can: 'sway her house, command her followers, / Take and give back affairs and their dispatch, / With such a smooth, discreet, and stable bearing' (Act 4 Sc 3). He finds her impressive, and her capabilities contribute to the swiftness with which he decides to accept her offer of marriage – note that she proposes to him. Her determination to pursue Cesario's hand in marriage and her willingness to make the first move say much for her strong and resolute character.

Orsino

"A noble Duke, in nature as in name."

This is a judgement made by the Captain, and we need to keep it in mind when considering the way Orsino is first presented. His love for music is plain from his opening words, but this love is bound up with the melancholy air he has when speaking of his love for Olivia: 'If music be the food of love, play on' (Act 1 Sc 1). It seems to be a pose: he is in love with the idea of being in love, and Olivia, with her decision to keep herself pure for seven years, is an ideal object for his unrealistic love.

Note that it is not until the very end of the play that he makes the decision to visit Olivia, when his presence is required to further the action. He quickly recognises that he does not really desire Olivia, but loves Viola once her real identity is known.

However, his positive attributes are recognised. Olivia, while rejecting his love, says of him: 'I suppose him virtuous, know him noble, / Of great estate, of fresh and stainless youth … A gracious person' (Act 1 Sc 5).

Orsino's words to Cesario, when he thinks he has been betrayed, are fierce: 'I'll sacrifice the lamb that I do love. / To spite a raven's heart within a dove' (Act 5 Sc 1), and the way he describes his love for Olivia: 'as hungry as the sea'. He ably rules his country, and we learn both from himself and from Antonio that he has taken part in battle: 'That face of his I do remember well. / Yet when I saw it last, it was besmeared / As black as Vulcan in the smoke of war' (Act 5 Sc 1).

At times, the language Orsino uses at the end of the play is in stark contrast to that he uses at the beginning: 'Kill what I love? – Savage jealousy … tear out of that cruel eye … my thoughts are ripe in mischief' (Act 5 Sc 1), and points towards a very different man than is suggested by his languid and relaxed opening pose.

Sebastian

"Most provident in peril "

It is, again, the Captain's testimony at the beginning of the play that sets out Sebastian's major characteristics. 'Provident in peril', 'courageous' and 'hopeful' also describe Viola's character, and underline the fact that, in character as well as looks, she is her brother's identical twin.

Sebastian is a man of action. When confronted by Sir Andrew's unprovoked attack, he responds swiftly and is willing to take on Sir Toby as well, giving an excellent account of himself. This swiftness of action and ability to judge people stands him in good stead when he meets Olivia. Startled by his reception, he nevertheless reacts quickly. He judges Olivia to be worthy, capable and beautiful, and agrees to marry her.

His reaction to Antonio when they at last meet again is obviously genuine. When he pledges his love to Olivia, 'And having sworn truth, ever will be true' (Act 4 Sc 3), we feel he will be as good as his word.

Sir Toby Belch

Sir Toby is a man of contradictions. His last name, Belch, is a good indicator of his personality, for it sums up his drunken, overlarge nature in a particularly unflattering way.

Virtually every time we meet Sir Toby in the play, he is <u>drinking and enjoying</u> himself. He is also <u>quick-witted</u>, as is seen in his conversations with Sir Andrew, Maria, Feste and Malvolio, in which he holds his own, with <u>swift</u> <u>repartee</u>.

There is, however, a down side to his character, apart from his drunken revels. The <u>callous</u> way he treats Sir Andrew in taking his money under the pretext of advancing his cause with Olivia, and in <u>making fun</u> of him both to his face and behind his back, does not endear him to us. Neither does the way he treats Malvolio – it is his idea to have him locked up as a madman, showing that he has a <u>cruel side</u>.

Sir Toby represents the <u>low comedy</u> of *Twelfth Night*. As such he generates much of the play's <u>humour and energy</u> and provides a <u>contrast</u> to the courtly love affairs of the main plot.

Feste

As the one person who <u>moves freely</u> between all groupings of characters, and between main and subplot, Feste is ideally placed both to <u>comment on the action</u> and to help it along. The <u>professional fool</u> of the play, as distinct from 'real' fools like Sir Andrew and Malvolio, he observes that: 'Foolery, sir, does walk about the orb like the sun, it shines everywhere' (Act 3 Sc 1).

But perhaps Feste is most <u>associated with music</u>. Whether singing love songs for Orsino or revels for Sir Toby, his love of music comes across clearly. What he has to <u>say in his songs</u> is also important.

He is a <u>shrewd commentator</u> on character and action. He takes Olivia to task for the time she intends to spend in mourning for her brother, 'proving' the folly of her actions. His comments about the Duke's mind being like 'taffeta ... and opal' sum up aspects of

Orsino's character. Of Sir Andrew he comments: 'Better a witty fool than a foolish wit' (Act 1 Sc 5). Perhaps it falls to Viola to sum up Feste accurately: 'This fellow is wise enough to play the fool; / And to do that well craves a kind of wit' (Act 3 Sc 1). He plays the fool well, but he is no fool.

Malvolio

Malvolio creates a range of responses in the audience. On the one hand he is a most unlovable, pretentious character; on the other he has our sympathy for the way he is treated by Sir Toby and Maria. He is a Puritan, a person with excessively strict views about morality. A man of his views is bound to come into conflict with Sir Toby.

Olivia values his services as a steward, and when she comes to the conclusion that he is ill, she commands: 'Let some of my people have a special care of him: I would not have him miscarry for the half of my dowry' (Act 3 Sc 4). Olivia does, however, recognise his major failing, one that Maria takes full advantage of in the subplot: 'O, you are sick of self-love, Malvolio, and taste with a distempered appetite' (Act 1 Sc 5). It is Maria who puts his foolish streak of self-love into clear language: 'the best persuaded of himself, so crammed, / as he thinks, with excellencies, that it is his grounds / of faith that all that look on him, love him' (Act 2 Sc 3). This is perhaps why he cannot get on with the servants, Sir Toby or Maria. It also goes some way to explain his churlish behaviour to Viola when he throws Olivia's ring on the ground, and his very foolish view that he might one day be Olivia's husband: even before he received the letter he was playing out that particular fantasy.

Sir Andrew Aguecheek

For once it is not the Captain who provides information on a character, but Maria. She says of Sir Andrew: 'he's a fool, he's a great quarreller' (Act 1 Sc 3) – not a flattering portrait, but then Sir Andrew does not appear to be a very attractive character at all.

In his foolishness, he blindly follows everything Sir Toby suggests and believes everything he says. On the one occasion he makes a sensible suggestion, that Sir Toby would have gained the best of the duel if he had not been drunk; the reward he gets from Sir Toby is to be called 'An asshead, and a coxcomb, and a knave – a thin-faced knave, a gull!' (Act 5 Scene 1), which is perhaps the best description of Sir Andrew Aguecheek.

The ease with which Sir Toby parts him from his money shows Sir Andrew to be a fool. However, he serves a useful purpose in the play. He is a foil for Sir Toby, in words, appearance and action. His foolish love for Olivia parallels Malvolio's similarly foolish hope. His cowardly attack on frightened Cesario and then on not-so-frightened Sebastian provide moments of humour and light relief.

Servants and Sea Captains

Among the many other servants and courtiers, only Maria is a thoroughly distinctive character. Her major contribution to the action is in devising the plan to make a fool of Malvolio. As such, she contributes to the humour and comic success of the subplot.

She can be sharp-tongued, as when she greets Viola (Act 1 Sc 5), and when she takes delight in making fun of Sir Andrew (Act 1 Sc 3). However, her devising of the plot against Malvolio shows her at her best. She thinks of the plot, writes the letter and ensures that

Malvolio will find it. It is Maria who suggests that Feste should disguise himself as Sir Topas, the curate, to confuse Malvolio even more.

Fabian appears as a part-time member of the gang of revellers, and joins in several key scenes. His rank in Olivia's house is obscure. Though more restrained than the others, he is skilled with language and delights in folly – surely not another jester?

The two Sea Captains, Antonio and Viola's anonymous helpers, occupy similar and essential roles in introducing the twins to Illyria and to the audience. Antonio's further involvement (the purse, the duel, etc.) is dictated by his love for Sebastian.

William Shakespeare

William Shakespeare was born in Stratford-upon-Avon on 23 April 1564. His father, John Shakespeare, was a glove-maker by trade and a respected member of the community, holding, at various times, several important public offices, including those of councillor, Justice of the Peace and, in 1568, Mayor. Besides his craft as a glove-maker, he was a successful businessman trading in wool and involved in money lending. Shakespeare's mother, Mary Arden, was the daughter of a wealthy local farmer.

It is likely that, as the son of an important townsman, Shakespeare's education began at the town's 'petty' or junior school, before he went on to Stratford Grammar School, where he learned Latin and studied the classical writers, such as the Roman writers Ovid and Plautus. The influence of these writers can be seen in some of Shakespeare's plays, such as *Antony and Cleopatra* and *Julius Caesar*.

In 1582, when he was 18, Shakespeare married Anne Hathaway, the 26-year-old daughter of a local farmer. Their first child, Susanna, was born the following May and the twins, Judith and Hamnet, were born two years later. Sadly, though, Hamnet died in 1596 at the age of 11.

Very little is known about Shakespeare's life between 1585 and 1592, and these are sometimes known as 'The Lost Years'. We do know, however, that by 1592 he had moved to London. He probably left Stratford around 1586–7, and it seems likely that he joined one of the London-based theatre companies which sometimes visited the town. He would have known that London was the place to be if he wanted to become a successful actor/playwright. By 1592, Shakespeare had established his reputation as an actor and dramatist and was sufficiently well known to attract comment from some other dramatists of the time.

In 1593 all the theatres were closed because of the plague, and when they reopened the following year, Shakespeare had joined others to form a new theatre company under the patronage of the Lord Chamberlain, called The Lord Chamberlain's Men. Shakespeare wrote plays for this company for almost twenty years, and its leading actor, Richard Burbage, played many of the roles created by Shakespeare, such as Hamlet, Othello and King Lear.

In 1599 the Lord Chamberlain's Men built a new theatre, The Globe, on the south bank of the River Thames at Southwark, and Shakespeare was a major shareholder in this venture. In 1603, Elizabeth I died and James I (James IV of Scotland) came to the throne. Shakespeare's company changed its name to The King's Men, and in 1609 the company acquired another theatre, the Blackfriars, in addition to the Globe.

Shakespeare's success had made him a wealthy man, and as early as 1597 he had bought one of the biggest houses in Stratford – he kept close links with his home town even though he lived in London. Shakespeare's father had been granted a coat of arms in 1596, and after his father's death in 1601 Shakespeare inherited this and the rights of a gentleman, an unusual privilege for an actor or dramatist at the time.

During the early 1600s Shakespeare wrote some of his most famous tragedies including *Hamlet*, *Othello*, *King Lear* and *Macbeth*. His last plays, sometimes called the Romances, which include *Cymbeline*, *The Tempest* and *The Winter's Tale*, were written between about 1608 and 1612. About 1611 Shakespeare seems to have left London and retired to Stratford a wealthy man, though he kept up his connection with London as he was involved in a legal dispute over the Blackfriars theatre in 1615. He died in Stratford on 23 April 1616 and was buried there in the Holy Trinity Church.

Imogen Stubbs and Helena Bonham-Carter in the 1997 film adaptation

In Elizabethan England, theatre-going was very popular and, although the theatres themselves were in London, travelling theatre companies went round the country and were hired by those who wanted a play to be performed as an attraction. Often plays were performed in temporary theatres created in inn yards, as well as at court and in the country houses of the wealthy. The plays, therefore, were seen by a wide range of people from all kinds of social backgrounds.

By the end of the 16th century, theatre-going was well established in England, but the theatres of Shakespeare's time were very different from modern theatres. The majority of them, such as The Globe in Southwark, London, were open-air and, as there was no artificial lighting, the plays had to be performed in daylight, normally in the afternoons. The theatre itself was round or hexagonal in shape, and there was a raised platform that jutted out into the audience. There was a recess at the back of the stage, which was supported by pillars and roofed to form a kind of turret from which a trumpeter signalled the beginning of the play and from which a flag flew, indicating that a performance was in progress.

The stage had no curtain and the main part of the audience stood around it on three sides. This section of the audience was called the 'groundlings'. A few special members of the audience were allowed to sit on the stage itself. In the galleries looking down on the stage and the groundlings, seating was provided for those who paid more to watch the play. These were covered and so afforded protection from the weather.

At the back of the stage, a large tapestry or curtain was hung concealing a recess and openings at either side from which the actors could enter and exit. The hanging might be colourful or dark, depending on the mood of the play. The stage itself was covered by a canopy, which rested on posts or pillars at either side. There was one or more trap doors in the stage itself, through which actors could quickly appear or disappear when necessary, for example in the appearance or disappearance of a ghost.

Behind the stage there were rooms called 'tiring rooms', in which the actors dressed and stored their various items and such props as were used. Although 'costumes' as such were not used, and actors dressed in the fashions of the times, these clothes were often more colourful or ornate and striking than those worn for everyday living. Painted scenery was not used, although props such as tables, chairs, thrones, cauldrons, swords, daggers and so on were used. All the female roles were played by men, as women were not allowed on the stage in Shakespeare's time, so tall boys with high-pitched voices were often trained to take women's parts.

People saw the theatre not only as a place to watch and enjoy a play, but as an opportunity to meet friends, exchange gossip and eat and drink. During performances, beer was often drunk and vendors moved among the groundlings selling various foods and sweetmeats. Elizabethan audiences were appreciative of a good play performed well but, if the play or performance was poor, they would often shout out derogatory remarks, make jokes at the actors' expense and throw things onto the stage – behaviour that is rarely seen in the modern-day theatre.

Appearance and reality

This theme encompasses the idea of the discrepancy between appearance and reality, and mistaken identity. Disguise plays a major role in this. The disguise which leads to the most confusion in the play is, of course, that of Viola when she dresses as a man and calls herself Cesario. The disguise does indeed fool everyone. Orsino is taken in, though he does make reference to Cesario's pleasing looks and youth. Olivia is so taken in by Viola's disguise that she falls in love with Cesario and wants to marry 'him'. At the end of the play even Sebastian, Viola's brother, cannot quite believe his eyes and needs her to recount details from their childhood to prove her identity.

If it were a simple matter of Viola being disguised as a man there would be confusion enough but, because she is identical to her twin brother Sebastian, other mistakes follow. Viola's disguise deceives everyone, Sebastian is mistaken for Cesario, and more confusion follows when Cesario is mistaken for Sebastian.

There are two other incidents of mistaken identity, and both involve Malvolio. Malvolio cannot see through the disguise of Feste when he pretends to be Sir Topas, the curate. Given the darkness of the room and the fact that Feste changes his voice this is not, perhaps, remarkable. The other matter is of more importance. Malvolio fails to see through the forged handwriting of the letter Maria wrote. She disguises her handwriting to look like Olivia's, and Malvolio is completely deceived.

Love and friendship

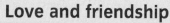

The play is about love but, fitting with the theme of mistaken identity, love comes in many guises.

Orsino and love

Orsino says he is in love with Olivia, but it is a pose. Olivia is merely a totem, representing the idealised object of his love. His romantic love lacks a real object and is therefore superficial. Viola quickly gains a place at Orsino's side and becomes his confidante. He admires Cesario's beauty, and his promise to Cesario that he may 'call his [Orsino's] fortunes thine' has an ironic though prophetic truth.

Finally, Orsino goes to plead his cause directly with Olivia. Her curt rejection of him causes some pain and anger and his speech is much more forceful, his language more brutal than before. He ends by threatening to 'sacrifice the lamb that I do love' (Act 5 Sc 1), his first overt reference to affection for Cesario. This is quickly overturned when he realises Cesario is a woman, and then he recognises the true meaning of those 'thousand times' when Cesario said to him 'Thou never shouldst love woman like to me' (Act 5 Sc 1). Now, Orsino is really in love.

Olivia and love

Olivia's love for her brother is, much like Orsino's love for her, false. Not in the sense that she does not really grieve his loss, but in that her vow to mourn for seven years, her sprinkling of the chamber with tears, and her wearing of a veil, are all pure theatricals, empty gestures that say nothing about her true grief. Perhaps the only real purpose they serve is to keep Orsino's own theatrical display of love at a distance.

However, the love she shows for Cesario is another matter. From the moment she first sets eyes on 'him' in Act 1 Sc 5, Olivia is in love. Swiftly rejecting Orsino's declarations of love, Olivia is far more concerned to know about Cesario – twice she asks about 'his' parentage. When Cesario leaves, Olivia sends a ring after 'him' by Malvolio, an excuse to tempt 'him' back. There can be no doubt of the strength of Olivia's love, even at this early stage. In Act 3 Sc 1, she declares her love for Cesario: 'Love sought, is good; but given unsought, is better.'

Unfortunately for Olivia, the love she seeks, Cesario's, is not for her. The love she gives unsought is not accepted. She is rejected, just as she has rejected the Duke. In contrast to Orsino's leisurely pursuit of her from a distance, Olivia sends for Cesario. In her anxiety she actually questions her own true love by suggesting that: 'youth is bought more oft than begged or borrowed' (Act 3 Sc 4), and wonders what she can 'bestow' (i.e. give) him to buy his love. She offers a jewel, and gains Cesario's promise to come again.

Viola and love

Of the three major characters who occupy much of the play, Viola's love is the most balanced and controlled. She loves her brother dearly but, unlike Olivia, Viola has neither the time nor the inclination to spend seven years in mourning.

Like her brother, she falls in love suddenly and, like Olivia, the love she seeks is not returned. She recognises her love, but does her duty to the man who is employing her, even though she (Viola) would rather be his wife. Her conversations with Olivia are dignified and beyond reproach in terms of the duty she owes Orsino. The intensity of the love she has for him is seen when she explains to Olivia how she would go in pursuit of her love: 'Make me a willow cabin at your gate, / And call upon my soul within the house' (Act 1 Sc 5). Unfortunately for Viola, she is never in a position to declare her love openly.

Sebastian and love

On our first acquaintance with Sebastian, in Act 2 Sc 1, we witness the unfettered friendship and love that he has inspired in Antonio, and the love that he gives in return. This is no foolish, romantic liaison, but the recognition of admirable traits in each other's character and the wish to share in each other's pains and pleasures. That Sebastian holds Antonio dear is witnessed in Act 5 Sc 1: 'How have the hours racked and tortured me / Since I have lost thee!'.

His swift acceptance of Olivia's love and proposal of marriage is perhaps surprising, but remember he is a man of decision, a quality he shares with his sister. Thus, his acceptance of Olivia and marriage do not really strike a discordant note.

Misguided love

Malvolio is the prime example here. In Olivia's words, he is 'sick of self-love'. His conceit is such that he is perfectly willing to believe Olivia is in love with him, and fools himself that he loves her. Maria's trick plays on his excessive self-love, making him an object of ridicule. Sir Andrew also suffers from misguided love for Olivia. Sir Toby encourages Sir Andrew's courtship of his niece in order to keep him near as a source of money.

Music

'If music be the food of love, play on' (Act 1 Sc 1). Music is integral to the play's atmosphere. Many scenes are supported and enhanced by the music that accompanies them, whether it be the rarefied climate of Orsino's court, or the excited revelry of Sir Toby's merrymaking. The play begins with instrumental music and ends with a song. In virtually every scene, music is mentioned, played or sung.

Viola suggests that her musical ability may gain her entrance to the Duke's court, and it does, as the Duke is fond of music. She says to Olivia that were she a suitor she would 'Write royal cantons of contemned love / And sing them loud even in the dead of night' (Act 1 Sc 5). Sir Toby's drunken revels are enlivened by music. Feste sings 'Hey Robin, jolly Robin' (Act 4 Sc 2) when he taunts Malvolio that 'she [Olivia] loves another'.

Feste sings three important songs in the play. The love song he sings for Sir Toby and Sir Andrew in Act 2 Sc 3 encourages the listener to grasp love while young, because 'what's to come is still unsure'. He also, prophetically, sings: 'Journeys end in lovers meeting' (Act 2 Sc 3). Both elements are relevant to the play's action and the theme of love. Feste's next song, for Orsino, presents a tragic view of life and love which fits the Duke's mood: 'Come away, come away, death, ... Sad true lover never find my grave, / To weep there! (Act 2 Sc 4). Feste's last song is sung directly to the audience. It is a knowing summary of human life, wiser than Feste's first song, but also sadder and more realistic. Growing up is not much fun.

Self-deception and self-discovery

Disguise and deception are key ideas in the play, but it is also full of characters who do not really understand themselves or their feelings. This can be seen when characters quickly change when the circumstances or situation changes, or when they are easily influenced by other people. For example, at the beginning of the play Orsino thinks that he is desperately in love with Olivia, but the shallowness of his feelings is soon revealed when he meets Cesario/Viola and becomes aware of what true love is. Similarly, Olivia is in mourning for her dead brother and intends to isolate herself for seven years, but she soon discovers her true feelings when she meets Cesario/Viola and then finds Sebastian. Other characters have varying degrees of self-awareness and experience varying degrees of self-discovery as the plot develops. Sir Andrew, for example, has no idea how he is seen by the other characters and is in a deluded state throughout the play, and Malvolio has a completely misguided self-image when he thinks that Olivia could be in love with him. Feste, on the other hand, is the character who is, perhaps, more self-aware than any of the others and sees things for what they are.

Wit and Humour

As a comedy, wit and humour play an important part in *Twelfth Night*. They come in several forms. Malvolio is at the centre of much of the humour that is provoked at his expense. His vanity, his puritanical, kill-joy nature and his aspirations as a social climber make him a clear target for the likes of Sir Toby, so he is made the object of the audience's derision through the letter plot, which is not only designed to fool him, but to fool him using his own characteristics. It works because he has such an inflated view of himself and this, of course, adds much to the comedy.

Sir Andrew is also made the butt of the comedy, and his short-comings are similarly exposed for the audience's amusement.

The word-play of Feste also adds to the comedy, although his contribution is of a different kind. He acts as a mocker of absurdity and is a commentator, for the audience, on the follies of others.

Disorder

In a very real sense the subplot, which deals with the fooling and imprisonment of Malvolio, acts as a counterpoint to the main plot. In the main plot we are concerned with higher things: the loves of Viola, Orsino, Olivia and Sebastian. The language and style of presentation supports the romantic atmosphere. In contrast, the subplot is a boisterous, disorderly revel. Even where the subplot mimics the main plot in terms of love affairs, disorder prevails. The antics of Malvolio and Sir Andrew are the antithesis of proper courtship. Even the one marriage in the subplot, of Sir Toby and Maria, seems to happen as if by chance, as an afterthought.

However, disorder (in the sense of 'things turned upside down') prevails not just in the subplot, but throughout the play, until the final scene when quarrels and misunderstandings end, and the Duke and Olivia face reality. Viola resumes her true gender and Malvolio is freed with a chance of revenge. This is in keeping with the theme of Twelfth Night, the last of the twelve days of Christmas celebrations before normality returns. It is thought that the play was first performed (possibly actually on January 6th – the twelfth night) at the Middle Temple, one of the Inns of Court, which always celebrated Christmas with a Court of Misrule. A Lord of Misrule presided, instead of the dignitaries of law and the Church, and order was turned upside down during the revels. So, in the play, identities and sexes change, the Duke fails to enforce order, the Puritan steward is overthrown and a clown (the Lord of Misrule) becomes a Priest. Finally, order returns and the clown sings a sad little song of maturity.

Text commentary

Act I

Scene 1

> **"If music be the food of love, play on"**

<u>Music</u> has an <u>important</u> <u>role</u> in the play because it is a backdrop to much of the action. Given that <u>love</u> <u>is</u> <u>a</u> <u>major</u> <u>theme</u>, music can, in Orsino's words, be 'the food of love'. The importance of music is <u>emphasised</u> by the play opening with musicians playing, and closing with Feste's song: 'When that I was a little tiny boy'.

In the opening words of this first scene, Orsino speaks some of the most famous of Shakespeare's lines, lines which speak of the <u>intensity</u> <u>of</u> <u>his</u> <u>love</u> (for Olivia) and use the imagery of <u>music</u> <u>as</u> <u>a</u> <u>food</u>. The Duke's phrasing is rather <u>artificial</u> <u>and</u> <u>his</u> <u>language</u> <u>is</u> <u>self-consciously</u> <u>flowery</u>, which alert us to the fact that he pretends passion.

Explore

Look closely at the music image in the play's first speech. Dying, flowers and sweetness will all return in his last speech in this scene.

Love is the central theme of the play. Note how swiftly characters fall in love and, just as swiftly, marry. The words 'Even in a minute: so full of shapes is fancy / That it alone is high fantastical' give some indication that in matters of love, things are <u>not</u> <u>always</u> <u>as</u> <u>they</u> <u>seem</u>.

The reference to the sea in Orsino's first speech links with the events which follow, as it is the aftermath of the shipwreck involving Sebastian and Viola which gives rise to <u>confusions</u> <u>of</u> <u>identity</u> later in the play.

"But like a cloistress she will veiled walk"

Having learned of Orsino's love for Olivia, we quickly discover that it has been <u>rejected</u> and that she intends to remain secluded for seven years, in remembrance of her dead brother. Such a length of mourning is excessive, but in a way it <u>parallels</u> <u>that</u> <u>excess</u> <u>of</u> <u>love</u> shown by Orsino. Keep their attitudes in mind when you meet Viola, and contrast her robust reaction to the loss of her brother.

Explore

Is there something morbid about Orsino's and Olivia's words? Olivia is 'season[ing] a ... dead love'; Orsino puns on 'heart' and 'hart', a deer which is pursued to death.

Note how, in this first scene, later events and ideas are rehearsed: frustrated love, the death of a brother, the pervasive influence of music, reference to the sea, and the <u>difference</u> <u>between</u> <u>appearance</u> <u>and</u> <u>reality</u> – is Orsino really in love with Olivia, or does he only think he is? How real is Olivia's determination to mourn her dead brother for seven years? Are these two people disguising their true feelings? There is no simple answer at this stage, but <u>seeds</u> <u>of</u> <u>doubt</u> are sown here which are developed in later events.

Act 1 Scene 2

Although Viola fears that her brother may be dead, the Captain describes how, when he last saw Viola's brother, Sebastian was striving to save himself. Thus <u>there</u> <u>is</u> <u>hope</u> that he, like Viola, might have survived the shipwreck.

The ship's captain sketches in for Viola, and the audience, the affairs of Illyria with regard to Orsino and Olivia. He gives <u>more</u> <u>details</u> of Olivia's bereavement: her father died, leaving her in the care of her brother who died shortly after. Olivia's vow of

Text commentary

Explore

Note how the death of Olivia's brother is mirrored here by the possible loss of Viola's brother, Sebastian.

seclusion is recounted again: 'she hath abjured the company / And sight of men'.

The Captain is an <u>excellent</u> <u>character</u> <u>witness</u>. He gives testimony of the <u>courage</u> <u>and</u> <u>determination</u> of Sebastian when faced with imminent death in the shipwreck. He praises Olivia as a 'virtuous maid' and the Duke Orsino as a man of <u>stature</u> <u>and</u> <u>nobility</u>. Thus he encourages the audience to like these characters before they appear on stage.

Viola finds Orsino's bachelorhood of interest. Note that Viola already knew of Orsino, and she refers to the fact that 'he was a bachelor then'. The Captain confirms that this was still the case just a month before this shipwreck. Viola's awareness that the Duke is not married will shortly turn into something more.

Viola's almost <u>melancholy</u> wish that she might 'serve that lady' (Olivia) and perhaps participate in her sadness – as they both mourn brothers – until her own circumstances are improved, is quickly pushed aside. Viola is a <u>positive</u> <u>character</u>, in <u>contrast</u> to Olivia and Orsino (note how the latter waits until the very last Act before confronting Olivia herself with his love). She has a robust reaction to her loss, taking action to <u>improve</u> <u>her</u> <u>situation</u>: she will disguise herself as a man, seek employment, and hold on to the hope that her brother is still alive.

> *Conceal me what I am.* 99

Viola determines to seek employment in Orsino's household, disguised as a man. This is the first reference to the <u>theme</u> <u>of</u> <u>disguise</u>, or appearance and reality. It will be returned to on many other occasions as it is central to the action of the main plot, which turns on instances of <u>mistaken</u> <u>identity</u>.

Note how Viola emphasises that music will help her gain entrance to the Duke's service: 'I can sing / And speak to him in many kinds of music'. This again stresses the importance of music as a theme in the play. This second scene ends as the first began, with references to music, bringing the introduction of the main plot to an end. In the next scene the subplot is introduced.

The Captain, who appears to be a solid and unbiased witness, comments on various main characters:

- Sebastian is 'provident in peril' and demonstrates 'courage and hope';
- Orsino is 'A noble Duke, in nature as in name';
- Olivia is 'fair' and 'a virtuous maid'.

Note how Viola's actions in this scene show her to be very similar in character to her twin, Sebastian. By determining to seek employment, disguising herself as a man, and by her hopeful attitude towards her brother's survival, she also shows herself to be courageous and hopeful.

Act 1 Scene 3

❝Shall we set about some revels?❞

'I am sure care's an enemy to life' – Sir Toby suggests that his niece's vow is interfering with his own style of living, but equally it is relevant to how Olivia's vow is an 'enemy' to her own enjoyment of life – it takes the arrival of Cesario to change her attitude.

We have stepped 'downstairs' here. The poetry of the first two scenes, with references to love, music, passion, flowers and sorrow is replaced by much more down-to-earth style of conversation.

Sir Toby is a drunkard who <u>enjoys</u> <u>revelry</u>. The disorder he creates is in marked contrast to the harmony sought by the main characters. We learn from Maria how Olivia is upset by Sir Toby's 'ill hours', i.e. his late-night drinking.

> **❝ he's a very fool and a prodigal ❞**

Maria reports Olivia's impressions of Sir Andrew Aguecheek – a <u>'foolish knight'</u> – an accurate judgement. Note also Maria's assessment of him: 'fool', 'great quarreller' and 'coward'. Sir Toby's attitude to Sir Andrew is <u>contemptuous</u>: he openly makes fun of him, and shows how foolish he is. The description of him as a <u>quarreller</u> prepares us for when, later, he is persuaded to duel with Viola.

Explore

Note how in the first two scenes the lines are in verse: here, the conversation is in prose, emphasising the contrast between the characters involved and their concerns. What contrasting effects are created by the use of prose and poetry?

Humour is both deliberate and accidental, the latter in Sir Andrew's <u>innocent</u> <u>account</u> of himself: 'I am a great eater of beef and I believe that does harm to my wit … Oh, had I but followed the arts!' Sir Andrew's conversations with Maria and Sir Toby show him to be <u>foolish</u> <u>and</u> <u>vain</u>. He is easily persuaded to change his mind when he considers leaving for home and giving up his pursuit of Olivia.

It is obvious that Sir Toby does not really believe his niece will consider Sir Andrew as a prospective husband, and that he values Sir Andrew <u>only</u> <u>for</u> <u>the</u> <u>money</u> he can get from him for drink and as a <u>butt</u> <u>for</u> <u>his</u> <u>humour</u>. His claims for Sir Andrew are immediately disproved: the accomplished linguist ('three or four languages') is completely floored by 'pourquoi'. Sir Andrew's own claims for himself are very modest.

Scenes with Sir Toby and his friends are usually <u>spoken</u> <u>in</u> <u>prose</u>. Verse is <u>reserved</u> for the affairs of <u>Olivia, Orsino, Viola and Sebastian</u>. We have now been introduced to three very different

Explore

Investigate for yourself what talents Sir Andrew thinks himself to have (also what excuses he makes for his failings).

groups of characters, and the language each group uses is correspondingly different:

● At Orsino's court, the Duke speaks in verse and uses flowery, poetic imagery.

● The language spoken by Viola and the Captain is plainer as they are communicating and receiving information, but they speak verse as characters of some nobility.

● Sir Toby speaks in prose and his language is full of robust vigour and energy. He is clearly intelligent and bandies words with Maria. His jokes are crude: 'Good Mistress Accost ... "accost" is front her, board her, woo her, assail her.'

Act 1 Scene 4

Text commentary

> *I have unclasped
> To thee the book even of my secret soul.*

The swiftness of Cesario's advancement, 'He hath known you but three days, and already you are no stranger' and her question, 'Is [Orsino] inconstant, sir, in his favours?', suggest that already a bond is growing between the two, although there is as yet no indication that they are in love with one another. Of course, the fact that Viola is disguised as a man will put a barrier to such a relationship developing. Her question about Orsino's constancy perhaps shows she is already attracted to him and hopes his love for Olivia may not last.

Orsino has told Cesario all the most private secrets of his soul – his faith and trust in her are remarkable considering their short acquaintance, but they lay the foundation for his sudden realisation later in the play that he loves her.

Ironically, Orsino refers to Cesario's youthful appearance and his resemblance to a maid: 'they shall belie thy happy years /

That say thou art a man'. This irony is further emphasised in Orsino's last lines of the scene, when he suggests Cesario might eventually 'call his [Orsino's] fortunes thine.'

Remarkably these words are addressed to a 'male': 'Diana's lip / Is not more smooth and rubious'. The sexual confusion was no doubt aided by boys playing female parts.

Viola has a problem. She will carry out Orsino's instructions, but she has already decided that she would like to be his wife. Thus the first of the complicated love affairs is set in motion. Viola loves Orsino who, though attracted to her, is distracted from loving her because of her disguise as a man. However, Viola must disguise her love as she has the task of pleading his love for Olivia.

Act 1 Scene 5

> **I marvel your ladyship takes delight in such a barren rascal**

The initial part of the scene, involving Maria and Feste, provides light-hearted and witty conversation, in contrast to the intensity of Orsino telling of his love for Olivia in the previous scene.

Feste is an interesting character who moves freely between the various groupings: Orsino, Olivia and Sir Toby. However, he also keeps his distance – he is not really close to anyone in the play. Being a professional fool, with the task of being witty and amusing, is a precarious job.

When Feste asks permission to prove that Olivia is a fool, he shows himself to be more clear-thinking than Olivia, pointing to the inconsistency of her mourning her dead brother for so long when she believes he is in heaven. His frankness is not welcomed by Malvolio, and their brief conversation gives Feste the opportunity to <u>rebuke</u> <u>Malvolio</u> <u>sharply</u>, repeating Sir Toby's opinion – <u>he</u> <u>is</u> <u>a</u> <u>fool</u>.

We are warned not to be taken in by appearances, by those who appear wise. Feste himself, in a burst of Latin (the language of learning and the Church), says, 'Cucullus non facit monachum': 'A cowl doesn't make a monk.' Nor does a jester's motley make a fool!

66*Sick of self-love* 99

Olivia's comment to Malvolio that he is 'sick of self-love' is ironic. In a way, she suffers from the same fault: her mourning for her brother contains an element of self-pity. Her period of mourning actually lasts only a short time because she falls in love with Cesario. She is like Malvolio in another way too: she is proud, as Viola notes later in this scene.

Malvolio's position in Olivia's household <u>seems</u> <u>assured</u>, but it appears that he <u>does</u> <u>not</u> <u>command</u> <u>her</u> <u>respect</u>, nor that of anyone else. The ground is thus prepared for us to accept his downfall when it comes.

66*Madam, yond young fellow swears he will speak with you.*99

Malvolio's report of how Cesario had an answer for all his reasons as to why 'he' should not be admitted to see Olivia indicates 'his' quick wit and determination. This intrigues Olivia, who agrees to see Cesario.

Olivia's decision to use a veil to 'disguise' her face is quickly <u>replicated</u> in effect by Cesario's ironic comment that '<u>I</u> <u>am</u> <u>not</u> <u>that</u> <u>I</u> <u>play</u>'. The theme of disguise, for whatever reason, <u>frequently</u> <u>occurs</u> in the play. Olivia's comment that Cesario's words are 'like to be feigned' continues the theme. Note also how the references to 'sail', 'swabber' and 'hull' repeat the image of the sea and remind us of how Cesario came to be here, acting as Orsino's messenger. Cesario's comment, 'what I am and what I would are as secret as maidenhood', is an <u>ironic</u> reference to Viola's disguise.

In a very generous speech, 'Your lord does know my mind … a gracious person …', Olivia praises Orsino: he is <u>virtuous, noble, of great estate, learned, valiant,</u> etc. Cesario's response is to tell Olivia how, were he in the Duke's place, he would be able neither to understand her rejection, nor accept it. Intrigued, she asks what he (Cesario) would do in that position.

66 *Make me a willow cabin* 99

One of the most moving verses in the play, Cesario's words <u>have a great effect</u> on Olivia and perhaps explain the interest she takes in Cesario. Certainly, Olivia's questions about Cesario's background and her <u>willingness to see Cesario again</u>, with the slight <u>excuse</u> of desiring to know how Orsino will take another rejection of his love, indicate a greater than normal interest in this messenger. This is confirmed immediately after Cesario's exit, when Olivia repeats some of the information she has gleaned about Cesario. Her words, 'I feel this youth's perfections… creep in at mine eyes', confirm the impact that Cesario has had.

66 *I do I know not what* 99

The speed with which Olivia falls in love <u>is matched by other incidents</u> in the play. Viola already has <u>affection</u> for Orsino, as does he for 'Cesario': later, Sebastian will as quickly learn to love Olivia. But here, the <u>impetuous nature</u> of Olivia is seen when she sends Malvolio after Cesario with a ring which she says Cesario has left behind, and which she is determined that Cesario shall need to return. We ought to remember here Feste's comment that Olivia's long period of mourning for her brother **made no sense**. The **truth** of his words was obvious, and the swift development of Olivia's interest in Cesario makes us wonder how meaningful her mourning was.

The main plot – Olivia's love for Cesario and Viola's for Orsino – has been set in motion. The **complications** caused by Viola's disguise and her similarity to her brother Sebastian (yet to appear) have their origins here.

The subplot and its **relationships are established**. The theme of disguise (the difference between appearance and reality) will play a major part here, as in the main plot.

Note the contrast between the **revelry and disorder** of the subplot, and the **romance** of the main plot. This is reflected in the language used and in the style of conversation: verse for the main plot, prose for the subplot. In Scene 5, the opening humorous exchanges between Olivia and the 'rude' youth, Cesario, are in prose, changing to verse for the romantic speeches.

Quick quiz 1

Uncover the plot

Delete two of the three alternatives given, to find the correct plot.

1   In Illyria/Elysium/Messina, the Duke Curio/Orsino/Cesario is in love with Olivia/Viola/Maria, who will see no one, following the death of her lover/father/brother.

2   The shipwrecked Olivia/Viola/Maria disguises herself as a servant called Fabian/Feste/Cesario.

3   After only three/six/seven days, 'he' is already the Duke's confidant, and is sent to woo Olivia/to sing to Olivia/to make his fortune.

4   Olivia is attracted to 'the youth' – while 'he' already loves Valentine/Antonio/Orsino.

5   Meanwhile, Sir Toby and Maria/Feste/Curio tease the foolish Sir Andrew Agueface/Aguecheek/Belch.

What? Why? How? Where? When?

Find the line and complete the phrase or sentence.

1   What does Olivia say will take the sting out of a fool's insults?

2   What does Quinapalus say?

3   Why does Orsino think Cesario will have better luck with Olivia?

4   How does Orsino love Olivia, according to Cesario?

5   Where does Viola say her brother is, and what does this mean?

6   When was Sir Andrew planning to leave, for how long is he persuaded to stay, and why?

Who said that?

1   Who says: 'How will she love when the rich golden shaft/Hath kill'd the flock of all affection else'?

2   Who says: 'For I can sing/And speak to him in many sorts of music'?

3   Who says: 'I am sure care's an enemy to life'?

4   Who says: 'I marvel your ladyship takes delight in such a barren rascal'?

5   Who says: 'O, you are sick of self-love, Malvolio, and taste with a distemper'd appetite'?

Act 2

Act 2 Scene 1

> **The gentleness of all the gods go with thee**

This scene echoes Act 1 Sc 1: we are told who Sebastian is, his relationship to Viola, that they are twins, that Viola is beautiful and intelligent ('she bore a mind that envy could not but call fair'), and that Sebastian has been shipwrecked on the same shore as Viola. Like Viola, he determines to go to Orsino's court.

> **If you will not murder me for my love,
> let me be your servant.**

The relationship between Sebastian and Antonio reminds us of that <u>between Viola and the Captain</u>, although this relationship is clearly <u>deeper</u> because Antonio is willing to put himself in danger for Sebastian. Antonio's decision to follow Sebastian <u>in spite of danger to himself</u> is important, as he will contribute to the confusions which arise from the similarity between Sebastian and Viola.

Explore

Think about what Antonio's decision here tells you about his relationship with Sebastian. What problems might his decision cause?

Like his sister, Sebastian is obviously <u>liked</u> by his companions and is <u>generous in spirit</u>. He has <u>inspired so much affection</u> in Antonio that the latter is willing to follow him anywhere: 'I do adore thee so, / That danger shall seem sport'.

Act 2 Scene 2

> **Fortune forbid my outside have not charmed her.**

Malvolio is obviously unhappy at having to pursue Cesario with the ring, but he reports Olivia's message accurately. However, his <u>rudeness</u> to Cesario, who has done him no harm, helps to <u>prejudice</u> the audience against him so that when he suffers, later in the play, there is not much sympathy for him.

Viola recognises that Olivia has been <u>fooled</u> <u>by</u> <u>her</u> <u>disguise</u> and of that disguise she says: 'I see thou art a wickedness, / Wherein the pregnant enemy does much.' She can <u>sympathise</u> with Olivia as she herself has the same problem with Orsino. At the end of Act 1 Sc 2, Viola decided to leave the future for 'time' to sort out. Here she again decides that 'time, thou must untangle this, not I'.

Explore

What kind of knot is it that Viola says 'time must untangle'?

Time will indeed lead to the unravelling of the 'wickedness' that arises from disguise. That there is <u>much</u> <u>to</u> <u>sort</u> <u>out</u> is clear – Viola loves Orsino, who loves Olivia, who loves Cesario (Viola in disguise).

Act 2 Scene 3

> **❝Is there no respect of place, persons, nor time in you?❞**

Explore

What further examples of this foolishness you can find?

Those <u>excesses</u> which Sir Toby demonstrated in Act 1 Sc 3 are again shown here. His determination to <u>eat,</u> <u>drink</u> <u>and</u> <u>enjoy</u> <u>himself</u> confirms him as a lover of the good life. Sir Andrew's <u>foolishness</u> is shown in many ways. He is <u>unduly</u> <u>impressed</u> by Feste's invention of nonsense words ('Pigrogromitus', 'the Vaptians', 'Queubus') and finds his latest outburst of nonsense 'the best fooling'. Rather touchingly he constantly hints at his own foolishness: 'I do it more natural' (i.e. like a fool).

Feste takes part in this scene, but he is <u>not</u> <u>really</u> <u>one</u> <u>of</u> <u>them</u> – it has already been noted that he moves easily between the major groups of characters. His position as a <u>paid</u> <u>jester</u> is clear. Sir Toby and Sir Andrew fool for fun;

he looks for money. He sings a song to order after the knights have paid him sixpence (a tester) each, and last night he 'did impeticos thy gratillity' (pocketed Sir Andrew's tip). Here, his songs touch on the heart of the play: 'your true love's coming', and suggest that in the end all will be well: 'Journeys end in lovers meeting'. He also reminds us of Viola's comment that time will have to sort matters out: 'What's to come is still unsure'.

'O mistress mine, where are you roaming?' is a song that touches on many of the play's themes. Note also in this scene the catch, 'Hold thy peace, thou knave', and the song used to mock Malvolio.

Feste is the character who is most strongly linked to the theme of music and here we see how music, while contributing to the overall atmosphere of the scene, is also used to support the words and actions of other characters.

❝Have you no wit, manners, nor honesty…❞

Because he is a killjoy, Malvolio does not attract the audience's sympathy here, and so the plot against him is seen as a fair return. The fact that he is a Puritan also colours his view of Sir Toby's lifestyle. However, we should remember that he is Olivia's steward and it is his job to preserve her from Sir Toby's disorderly and disruptive behaviour.

Olivia dislikes Sir Toby's revelry and Maria suggests that he is in danger of being turned 'out of doors' for his noise. When Malvolio picks up this theme, it is not clear how far he is speaking for Olivia when he threatens that she is 'very willing to bid you farewell'.

Sir Toby's reminder to Malvolio that he is just a steward picks up his earlier comment to Maria, when he reminded her that he was 'consanguineous' (related by blood) to Olivia. He feels he has a special place in the household and that his position is unassailable. His rebuke to Malvolio, 'Dost thou think, because thou art virtuous, there shall be no more cakes and ale?' highlights the contrast between fun-loving Sir Toby and strait-laced Malvolio.

It is typical of Sir Andrew that he suggests challenging Malvolio to a duel after Malvolio has left the scene. It also foreshadows the time, later in the play, when he will be persuaded to duel with Cesario.

❝that vice in him will revenge find notable cause to work.❞

Maria's counsel to Sir Toby to desist from his revelry for the time being is sensible. She tells how Olivia is unhappy and distracted since Cesario visited her. However, her plan to hoax Malvolio is effective in gaining Sir Toby's quiet attention.

Maria's plan hinges on her ability to disguise her handwriting to appear like Olivia's and on Malvolio's foolish ambition to become Olivia's husband. She will suggest that Olivia loves Malvolio and would like to see him dressed in a way that, in reality, Olivia hates. She will drop the letter where Malvolio will surely find it, and Sir Toby and friends can enjoy the scene from safe hiding places.

Maria's plot to 'gull' Malvolio sets up many of the funniest scenes in the play. At first we feel no sympathy for Malvolio's suffering: he is an 'affection'd ass' whose conceit deserves it.

The plan having been laid and left in Maria's hands, she departs. The audience now gains new insight into Sir Toby's character. When Sir Andrew praises Maria, Sir Toby comments that she 'adores me'. However, his next words: 'what o' that?' are ungracious and selfish. They do not make him popular with the

Text commentary

audience and tend to <u>lessen</u> <u>any</u> <u>respect</u> <u>or</u> <u>liking</u> we may have had for him. The words also confirm Feste's accurate assessment in Act 1 Sc 5 when he suggested that if Sir Toby could get his senses together he would recognise Maria's talents. The other matter here is his quite open demand that Sir Andrew must obtain more money. His promise that Sir Andrew will marry Olivia in the end must fall rather flat on the audience's ears – he is obviously interested only in spending the money himself.

Sir Andrew's part in all this is <u>very</u> <u>foolish</u>: he takes part in the plot against Malvolio to see him humiliated before Olivia and blindly agrees to Sir Toby's demands for his money in the vain hope that he can buy Olivia's favour. Malvolio is a suitable victim: <u>pompous,</u> <u>overbearing,</u> <u>full</u> <u>of</u> <u>self-love,</u> <u>opinionated</u>, and a fool to himself in imagining Olivia could love him.

Act 2 Scene 4

> *Our fancies are more giddy and unfirm, …*
> *Than women's are.*

The re-entry of Orsino with his call, again, for music, <u>changes</u> <u>the</u> <u>tone</u> from revelry to that of love. Orsino's words echo the opening lines of the play. He senses that Cesario is in love and is surprised when told the woman involved resembles him and is about his age – this is as far as Viola <u>dare</u> <u>go</u> in declaring her love for Orsino. His advice to her – to choose a younger woman, as a man should be older than the one he loves – is <u>ironic</u>. In reality, Viola is in love with a man older than herself: Orsino!

There is a <u>seriousness</u> <u>about</u> <u>this</u> <u>scene</u>, shown by the return to verse and the call for music. Our first impression of Orsino is reinforced by the advice he gives to Cesario and his suggestion that women are like roses: their 'flower, being once displayed, doth fall that very hour' – <u>another</u> <u>affected</u> <u>pose</u>. It reminds us of the question we asked about Orsino in the first scene: is he really in love, or just playing at being in love?

❝ *I am slain by a fair cruel maid* ❞

Explore

What is the significance of Feste's song here?

Feste enters and is again asked to sing: his song speaks of the central theme of the play, love. It speaks of <u>unrequited</u> <u>love</u> (i.e. love that is given and not returned) which brings <u>unhappiness to the giver</u>. Orsino's love for Olivia is not returned, nor is Olivia's for Cesario, and nor is Viola's for Duke Orsino.

Feste again shows his <u>clear vision</u> of the characters of those around him. His comments that the Duke's tailor should make him a doublet of 'changeable taffeta'; and that the Duke's mind is 'a very opal' show that he views the Duke as a <u>changeable man whose mind is easily swayed</u>. The truth of this will be seen at the end of the play when Orsino suddenly switches his affection from Olivia to Viola, though to be fair by then he has spent much time in Viola's company and has always admired 'Cesario'.

The Duke is convinced that he understands love ('Make no compare / Between that love a woman can bear me / and that I owe Olivia'); yet we know he doesn't even understand the gender of his trusted messenger.

❝ *what love women to men may owe* ❞

Viola poses the problem that she faces in her love for the Duke. His suggestion that women cannot love to the same degree or with the same passion as men is <u>patently wrong</u>, given what we know of Viola. Viola's response is to defend the power of women's love, but she almost goes too far when she gives an example of woman's love: 'My father had a daughter loved a man — / As it might be perhaps, were I a woman'.

Viola's suggestion that <u>concealment of love</u> feeds 'like a worm i'the bud' to some extent echoes her earlier image: 'Disguise I see thou art a wickedness / Wherein the pregnant enemy does much (Act 2 Sc 2). Viola really loves the Duke, in <u>contrast to his sentimental imagining</u> of his love for Olivia.

The conclusion of this scene sees Cesario dispatched again to Olivia with a jewel to give her.

Act 2 Scene 5

> *I will smile, I will do everything that thou wilt have me.*

Fabian says that Malvolio is the reason that he (Fabian) is out of favour with Olivia, so he would 'exult' if Malvolio were made a fool of. Adding more information, Maria reports how Malvolio has been 'practising behaviour to his own shadow this half-hour', conjuring up a picture of Malvolio <u>preening himself</u>, his actions and movements, so that they will have the greatest effect on any future onlooker. These comments lessen the audience's sympathy for Malvolio and make him an <u>object of laughter</u>.

Explore

On stage, this is without doubt one of the funniest scenes in Shakespearean comedy. Why? The letter is pitched at a level which means that the audience knows that Malvolio will be taken in, but doing so shows how foolish and vain he is. How do the reactions of the observers (the plotters) help the comedy?

It is plain that Maria has <u>prepared Malvolio for the trick</u> because, as he wanders the garden talking to himself and rehearsing gestures and movements, he reflects on Maria's news that Olivia admires him. He begins to <u>convince himself</u> that Olivia gives him <u>more respect than she gives anyone else</u>. He <u>fantasises</u> about acting the lord of the manor, being gracious yet firm, calling for Sir Toby and telling him to stop getting drunk, and referring to Sir Andrew as a foolish knight. All of this is overheard with amusement but growing annoyance by Sir Toby, and it ensures that the audience has little sympathy with Malvolio when the trick is played.

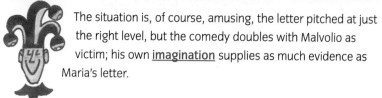

The situation is, of course, amusing, the letter pitched at just the right level, but the comedy doubles with Malvolio as victim; his own <u>imagination</u> supplies as much evidence as Maria's letter.

Malvolio 'recognises' the hand as Olivia's and goes on to suggest that he recognises individual letters. The letters M, O, A, and I have no special significance except that they are readily recognisable as forming part of Malvolio's name: enough for him to <u>interpret</u> <u>the</u> <u>letter</u> <u>as</u> <u>addressed</u> <u>to</u> <u>him</u>.

The letter's instructions are intended to <u>**convince**</u> <u>**him**</u> <u>**that**</u> <u>**it**</u> <u>**is**</u> <u>**genuine**</u>: they instruct him to behave much as he does at present ('Be opposite with a kinsman, surly with servants') and dress in a way that is sure to offend Olivia. Malvolio is <u>**completely**</u> <u>**taken**</u> <u>**in**</u>, convinced that the letter is from Olivia to him, and he <u>**resolves**</u> <u>**to**</u> <u>**do**</u> <u>**all**</u> <u>**it**</u> <u>**command**</u>s. The scene is set for his downfall.

When Malvolio departs, the onlookers <u>**express**</u> <u>**their**</u> <u>**delight**</u> that the plan has begun successfully. Sir Toby goes so far as to suggest that not only could he marry Maria for the <u>**ingenuity**</u> of her plan, he could also be her slave. This is a far cry from his last remark about Maria in Act 2 Sc 2, and is the <u>third</u> <u>reference</u> in the play to Sir Toby and Maria's possible marriage – the audience is <u>**well**</u> <u>**prepared**</u> <u>**for**</u> <u>**this**</u> <u>**event**</u>.

Maria confirms that Olivia will find Malvolio's behaviour unacceptable: she abhors the colour yellow, detests the fashion of cross-garters, and will find his ever-smiling face out of keeping with her melancholy mood.

Uncover the plot

Delete two of the three alternatives given, to find the correct plot..

1 *Malvolio gives Viola the ring: she realises that Orsino/Antonio/Olivia loves her, while she loves Orsino/Antonio/Cesario, and Orsino loves Cesario/Viola/Olivia.*

2 *The Duke sends for Feste/Curio/Cesario for music, and argues that men's love is weaker/stronger/more fickle than women's.*

3 *Meanwhile, the revellers are berated by Malvolio/Feste/Fabian for bear-baiting/fighting/singing.*

4 *A plan of revenge is devised by Maria/Feste/Sir Toby, whose voice/hand/handwriting is like Olivia's, to make Malvolio think Olivia wants to turn him out/marry him/turn out Sir Toby.*

5 *As the plan works, Toby admires Maria – echoed by Fabian/Feste/Sir Andrew.*

Who? What? Why? How?

1 *Who believes that all that look on him love him?*

2 *What 'gives a very echo to the seat/Where love is throned'?*

3 *What do journeys end in?*

4 *What three things persuade Malvolio that Olivia loves him?*

5 *Why did the song of the previous night relieve the Duke's passion much?*

6 *How had Malvolio been practising his behaviour?*

Who said that?

1 *Who modestly says: 'though it was said she much resembled me, [she] was yet of many accounted beautiful', and who is 'she'?*

2 *Who says: 'But come what may, I do adore thee so/That danger shall seem sport, and I will go'?*

3 *Who says: 'Have you no wit, manners, nor honesty, but to gabble like tinkers at this time of night?'?*

4 *Who says: 'If ever thou shalt love/In the sweet pangs of it remember me'; and why is this ironical?*

Act 3

Act 3 Scene 1

> **"** *Yet come again; for thou perhaps mayst move*
> *That heart, which now abhors, to like his love.* **"**

Cesario and Feste indulge in some <u>witty</u> <u>conversation</u> and word-play. Feste is respectful towards Cesario, but his remark about Cesario's need to grow a beard reminds Viola of <u>her love for Orsino</u>: she desperately wants a beard, but it belongs to Orsino; she does not want to grow one herself! When Feste leaves her, Viola muses on the difficult art of being a fool: 'a practice / As full of labour as a wise man's art'.

> **Explore**
>
> Look at Viola's comments about Feste. What does she think of him?

A brief conversation between Cesario, Sir Toby and Sir Andrew ensues. Cesario impresses in coping with the knights' attempts at courtly language. Sir Andrew, the linguist, attempts French, but withdraws when Cesario responds in the same language. Sir Toby attempts to confuse with <u>affected</u> <u>language</u>, but is met with bluntness and a parody of his own style: 'I will answer you with gait and entrance'. No wonder Sir Andrew, hearing Cesario's greeting to Olivia, finds him 'a rare courtier'.

From 'I prithee tell me what thou think'st of me' to 'Would it be better, madam, than I am?', Viola and Olivia spin a web of doubt about <u>disguised identity and disguised emotions</u>.

After some verbal sparring, during which Olivia cannot quite bring herself to speak her heart, she finally <u>declares her love for Cesario</u>: 'Cesario, by the roses of the spring, / By maidhood, honour, truth, and everything, / I love thee' (Act 3 Sc 1). Cesario's reply gives Olivia hope: no woman has or ever will be mistress of 'his' heart. As a woman, Viola knows this to be true. Her disguise <u>protects her</u> against violent attack, but creates <u>emotional</u> <u>confusion</u> for herself and th ose around her.

Act 3 Scene 2

> 66 *Will either of you bear me a challenge to him?* 99

Sir Andrew complains that Olivia is favouring Cesario far more than she ever did him. Fabian suggests that Olivia is doing this on purpose to make Sir Andrew jealous and to <u>fire</u> <u>up</u> <u>his</u> <u>passion</u>. Sir Toby persuades Sir Andrew that if he challenges Cesario to a duel and wins, Olivia will be impressed with his valour.

When Sir Andrew has left, Sir Toby says he will deliver Sir Andrew's challenge but does not think that the two will actually fight. He has a <u>low</u> <u>opinion</u> <u>of</u> <u>Sir</u> <u>Andrew's</u> <u>valour</u>: he has 'so much blood in his liver as will clog the foot of a flea'.

Maria arrives to confirm that Malvolio is following the letter's instructions and that they should witness the scene.

Act 3 Scene 3

> 66 *I would not by my will have troubled you,* *But since you make your pleasure of your pains,* *I will no further chide you.* 99

The reappearance of Antonio and Sebastian signals the next stage in the main plot. Antonio's love for Sebastian is reinforced: he wishes <u>to</u> <u>protect</u> <u>him</u> but, because he is a 'wanted man' in Illyria, he has to lie low. However, he offers Sebastian his purse, and it speaks highly of Sebastian's character that Antonio is <u>willing</u> <u>to</u> <u>risk</u> <u>so</u> <u>much</u> <u>for</u> <u>him</u>.

Explore

Disguise is not confined to Viola's appearance as Cesario. Viola is 'not what I am'; nor is Olivia. What about Olivia's last speech? Who is she deceiving: herself, Cesario, or both?

Text commentary

47

Explore

Think about the relationship between Sebastian and Antonio. How does it develop in this scene?

Coming immediately after Sir Andrew's decision to fight Cesario, Sebastian's reappearance prepares the ground for the problems of mistaken identity which have consequences in both the main and the subplots.

Act 3 Scene 4

> ❝*How shall I feast him? What bestow of him?* ❞

Olivia's first words show that she is very much in love with Cesario. To calm herself down, she calls for her 'sad and civil' servant Malvolio.

Viola is not the only character to appear transformed: Malvolio, deceived by his illusions, is now altered 'in very strange manner'. Olivia prays heaven to restore him to what he was.

> ❝*Some have greatness thrust upon them* ❞

When Malvolio arrives, smiling and cross-gartered, he attempts to engage Olivia in witty conversation. Olivia's suggestion that he should go to bed he takes to be an invitation to her bed. He knowingly quotes 'Olivia's' letter to her: her response is that he suffers from 'midsummer madness'. News of Cesario's arrival distracts her attention and she instructs Maria to place Malvolio in her servants' care.

Malvolio thinks Olivia's behaviour complies exactly with 'her' letter. His reason is blunted by his own fevered imaginings of his coming greatness.

Sir Toby, Maria and Fabian enjoy themselves hugely at Malvolio's expense. Sir Toby thinks his wits are affected: 'His very genius hath taken the infection of the device'. Fabian agrees: 'we shall make him mad indeed'. Sir Toby proposes binding Malvolio and

Text commentary

putting him into a dark room as though he were a madman: more fun at Malvolio's expense.

> ❝*Youth, whatsoever thou art, thou art but a scurvy fellow.*❞

Sir Andrew's challenge shows his foolishness: it makes little sense and will only confuse Cesario. Having encouraged Sir Andrew to his face, Sir Toby gives his real judgement on the letter once he has gone; it is 'excellently ignorant'. Praising Cesario's 'good capacity and breeding', Sir Toby says he will not deliver Sir Andrew's letter, because it will 'breed no terror' in Cesario. He determines to deliver the challenge by word of mouth. Note how he takes little account of the feelings of either Cesario or Sir Andrew – his only consideration is his own enjoyment.

Meanwhile Olivia has been declaring her love to Cesario, but has received no encouragement: 'I have said too much unto a heart of stone'. Viola demonstrates great loyalty to Orsino, in spite of her love for him and in the face of Olivia's declarations of love. It would perhaps have been easier for her to undermine Orsino's quest for Olivia's hand in order to improve her own chances with Orsino. But her integrity is such that she does the job Orsino has given her.

> ❝*That defence thou hast, betake thee to't.*❞

Explore

Note that the duel is important because it causes Antonio to mistake Viola for Sebastian and gives Viola hope that her brother might be alive.

Sir Toby accosts Cesario, warning that Sir Andrew intends to challenge 'him' to a duel. He declares that Sir Andrew has already killed three men: 'Souls and bodies hath he divorced three'. Cesario is reluctant ('A little thing would make me tell them how much I lack of a man') but, as Sir Toby's insistence, draws her sword.

When Cesario and Sir Andrew meet, the comedy of the situation lies in their mutual fear, which is understandable, given Sir Toby's efforts to disguise the reality of the situation from them both. This is another example of disguise confusing appearance and reality during the course of this long scene.

Hardly have swords been drawn when Antonio appears and, mistaking her for Sebastian, declares he will fight on Cesario's behalf. This is prevented by the arrival of officers of the peace, who arrest Antonio 'at the suit of Count Orsino'.

Antonio, bound for prison, asks Cesario for his (Antonio's) purse. Although confused, Viola volunteers to lend him half her money, regardless of their short acquaintance – another pointer to her generous character. Antonio is astounded, and the more he protests against 'Sebastian's' rejection of their friendship, the more puzzled Cesario becomes.

The influence of Sebastian is now felt, and Viola struggles to understand: 'I know of none, / Nor know I you by voice or any feature.'

When Antonio describes how he snatched his friend from the jaws of death, and addresses him as 'Sebastian', the first step is taken towards the unravelling of the misunderstandings caused by Viola's disguise. The fact that Antonio could mistake Viola for her brother Sebastian also lends credibility to the mistake that Olivia will shortly make in believing that Sebastian in Cesario.

The departure of Antonio with the officers leaves Viola to wonder alone. Denied the opportunity to question Antonio further, she can but hope: 'Prove true, imagination, O prove true ... O, if it prove / Tempests are kind, and salt waves fresh in love!'

> **If this were played upon a stage now, I could condemn it as an improbable fiction.**

Many of Shakespeare's plays build up to a climax during the first three acts, then level off during Act 4 before the major last act climax. Certainly the action so far peaks in Act 3 Sc 4, a lengthy scene of <u>enormous</u> <u>variety</u>.

The plot against Malvolio reaches its farcical high-point: as he <u>deludes</u> <u>himself</u> in his <u>vain</u> <u>and</u> <u>self-deceiving</u> <u>soliloquy</u> and sets about being rude to everyone, it is the last time we can enjoy his suffering without feeling an element of sympathy.

Another gloriously <u>farcical</u> <u>episode</u> is the duel between Sir Andrew and Cesario, neither with any appetite for combat, lured on by the lies and encouragement of Sir Toby. A nice contrast is the alacrity with which Antonio and Sir Toby draw their swords. This is the climax to another piece of trickery, but equally it leads towards the next stage of the drama, with Antonio's arrest and Viola's <u>awareness</u> <u>of</u> <u>Sebastian's</u> <u>survival</u>.

At the same time, Olivia's love is now openly revealed, and Cesario's rejection of her continuing declarations advances the main plot in between the rowdy comedy.

Sir Toby reduces each of the duellists to terror: 'Pray God defend me!', 'Pray God he keep his oath!' But the duel is interrupted. The various plots overlap with a <u>greater</u> <u>variety</u> <u>of</u> <u>characters</u> than anywhere except the last scene.

Uncover the plot

Delete two of the three alternatives given, to find the correct plot.

1   Cesario comes to return Olivia's ring/press the Duke's suit/declare his love.

2   Olivia declares her love for Orsino/Malvolio/Cesario.

3   Ignoring Sir Andrew's/Orsino's/Maria's letter, Sir Toby conveys challenges, telling each party that the other is a coward/devil/knight.

4   They are parted by Antonio/Sebastian/the Captain, who is arrested and, asking for his sword/purse/sea-cap, accuses Viola/Sir Toby/Olivia of ingratitude.

5   Viola realises he mistakes her for Cesario/Orsino/Sebastian.

Who? What? Why? How?

1   Who is 'sad and civil', and why is the comment ironic?

2   What was Antonio's crime against Orsino?

3   What is 'more matter for a May morning', and what was the previous 'matter'?

4   Why, according to Fabian, has Olivia shown favour to Cesario?

5   Why is Viola willing to give money to Antonio, and why does he expect it?

6   How does Sir Toby respond when Fabian remarks how 'dear' Sir Andrew has been to him?

Who said that?

1   Who says: 'I love thee so that, maugre all thy pride,/Nor wit nor reason can my passion hide'?

2   Who says: 'My willing love/The rather by these arguments of fear,/Set forth in your pursuit'?

3   Who says: Oh, if it prove,/Tempests are kind, and salt waves fresh in love'?

4   Who says: 'I have said too much unto a heart of stone'?

5   Who says: 'You are idle shallow things; I am not of your element'?

Act 4

Act 4 Scene 1

> *Let fancy still my sense in Lethe steep;*
> *If it be thus to dream, still let me sleep.*

The next stage in the discovery of Sebastian and the playing out of his part in the main plot now takes place. Sent by Olivia to bring Cesario to her, Feste has chanced upon Sebastian whom he mistakes for Cesario. Sebastian, much to Feste's surprise, denies that he is called Cesario or that he knows Feste's lady.

In the midst of their dispute they meet Sir Andrew and Sir Toby. Sir Andrew takes Sebastian by surprise and strikes him, being <u>under</u> <u>the</u> <u>impression</u> that he is addressing Cesario: another case of mistaken identity.

Sir Andrew, as ever, is no more capable of reasoning than fighting. Beaten by Sebastian, he decides to bring an action of battery though he was the first to attack. Sebastian's natural reaction is, 'Are all these people mad?'

The eruption of the fight between Sir Andrew and Sebastian is <u>not</u> <u>allowed</u> <u>to</u> <u>develop</u> into a serious affair involving Sir Toby. Olivia arrives and soundly berates and banishes Sir Toby, then turns her attention to Sebastian, whom she, too, mistakes for Cesario.

Explore

If you examine this scene and Scene 3, you should find about five occasions where Sebastian questions the sanity of the people of Illyria – or himself. However, he still responds instantly and boldly to all situations.

The arrival of Sebastian is the trigger for Olivia to seek her own enjoyment, not bury herself in melancholy. He agrees; she wastes no time: 'Would thou'dst be ruled by me!' O, say so, and so be.' She addresses him with <u>affection</u> and invites him into her house. Sebastian, though surprised and confused, is also delighted, and willingly agrees to be 'ruled' by her. His agreement is <u>happily</u> <u>received</u> by Olivia 'O, say so, and so be!'

Act 4 Scene 2

> **"** *I say there was never man thus abused. I am no more mad than you are.* **"**

Malvolio has been imprisoned in a dark room. Maria persuades Feste to <u>disguise</u> <u>himself</u> as Sir Topas, the curate, and to visit Malvolio. Instead of helping Malvolio, he taunts and confuses him, telling him he is not in a dark room but in a house that is full of light, finally concluding that Malvolio is mad and shall remain there until he (Sir Topas) is convinced he is sane.

Feste's <u>use</u> <u>of</u> <u>disguise</u> is a impressionist's virtuoso performance. 'God buy you, good Sir Topas – Marry, amen – I will, sir, I will.' Are we now uneasy about laughing at Malvolio's sufferings?

Sir Toby, however, is now afraid he might have gone too far and wishes for Malvolio to be released. He does not want to lose his position in Olivia's house. Malvolio at last prevails upon Feste to provide him with writing materials so that he can explain his behaviour to Olivia.

This is the stage of the play where the theme of the <u>Court</u> <u>of</u> <u>Misrule</u> is most evident. Coming in from outside, Sebastian sees the <u>world</u> <u>as</u> <u>mad</u>, and the clown takes on the role of the Priest. This is an entertaining scene, largely because of the foolery of Feste, giving an impression of a <u>pompously</u> <u>nonsensical</u> <u>priest</u> and inventing much dignified nonsense.

However, the taunting of Malvolio has taken on a <u>different</u> <u>mood</u> here. In this scene we gradually see that Malvolio

Explore

Find as many examples as you can of Feste's use of such contradictions and confusions. What do his increasingly rapid changes of character add to the humour?

has a case and become uneasy with the cruelty of the deception. The letter Malvolio is now allowed to write will show him to be <u>sane</u> and make his case to Olivia and Duke Orsino.

Act 4 Scene 3

> *Plight me the full assurance of your faith,*
> *That my most jealous and too doubtful soul*
> *May live at peace.*

Sebastian finds his situation almost <u>unbelievable</u> and has to convince himself that everything around him is real. He knows he is not mad and considers briefly whether Olivia is. However, he reasons that she would not be able to <u>command</u> <u>such</u> <u>a</u> <u>large</u> <u>household</u> <u>if</u> <u>she</u> <u>were</u> <u>mad</u>. One may wonder at Sebastian's behaviour. He is much more <u>impulsive</u> than his sister who, despite enormous temptation, has <u>not</u> <u>declared</u> <u>her</u> <u>love</u> for Orsino.

Olivia brings a priest to carry out the marriage ceremony and Sebastian agrees to marry her. It is not surprising that, as Sebastian seems willing to <u>accept</u> <u>her</u> <u>love</u>, Olivia acts quickly to seal their marriage. Rejected for so long by Cesario and having had sufficient time to test her own feelings about 'him', she moves with <u>decisiveness</u> when the opportunity presents itself.

Explore

Think about Sebastian's role in this scene. What are his main concerns? Why is he so willing to obey Olivia?

This crucial preparatory scene enables all the deceptions, disguises, riddles and mistakes to be <u>removed, solved or put right</u> in one almost ceremonial parade in the last act. Everything has to take its place in the unravelling. To reveal Cesario and Sebastian as two people too early would <u>spoil the unfolding</u>.

Text commentary

Quick quiz 4

Uncover the plot

Delete two of the three alternatives given, to find the correct plot.

1   Feste, sent to find Orsino/Cesario/Olivia, finds
    Sebastian/Antonio/Viola instead.

2   So does Sir Toby/Sir Andrew/Fabian, who follows up his threat by
    striking 'Cesario'. Sebastian hits back/draws his sword/throws his
    dagger.

3   Fabian/Feste/Maria dresses as Sir Toby/Sir Topas/Pythagoras, who
    confirms that Malvolio is mad – but Sir Toby is
    afraid/keen/embarrassed to carry the joke further.

4   Meanwhile, Sebastian, amazed that Olivia/Maria/Viola loves him,
    agrees to marry her/live at peace with her/celebrate with her.

Who? What? Why? How?

1   Who is an 'ungracious wretch/Fit for the mountains and the
    barbarous caves'?

2   Who does Sebastian wish to ask for advice, and why is this
    impossible?

3   What has Olivia given Sebastian, and what other occasions does this
    echo?

4   Why does Sir Toby decide to abandon his 'sport'?

5   Why are Sebastian and Sir Andrew both surprised by their encounter?

6   How does Olivia run her affairs?

Who said that?

1   Who says: 'I say there was never man thus abus'd'?

2   Who says: 'Then you are mad indeed, if you be no better in your wits
    than a fool.' – and to whom?

3   Who says: 'I'll... go with you,/And, having sworn truth, ever will be
    true'?

4   Who says: 'Blame not this haste of mine' – and why is this particularly
    striking to Sebastian?

5   Who says: 'I would we were well rid of this knavery'?

Act 5

Act 5 Scene 1

> *they praise me and make an ass of me*

It is very noticeable that Feste acts as a <u>professional</u> <u>clown</u> throughout the play. The scene with Orsino here is another example of his skilful begging for tips: compare it with a similar scene with Viola in Act 3 Sc 1. You can also find other references to his being paid for his work. That is why, of course, he <u>belongs</u> <u>to</u> <u>no</u> <u>faction</u>, though employed by Olivia: he will jest or sing for whoever pays him and the only constant is his <u>opposition</u> <u>to</u> <u>the</u> <u>Puritan</u>, Malvolio.

> *here comes the Countess:*
> *now heaven walks on earth.*

Explore

What does Orsino have to say to Feste here? Why do you think Shakespeare included this conversation at the beginning of the scene?

So far, Orsino's courtship of Olivia has been done through Cesario. Now he takes matters into his own hands. With all the main characters assembled, the <u>misunderstandings</u> <u>can</u> <u>finally</u> <u>be</u> <u>resolved</u>. Orsino's conversation with Feste <u>lightheartedly</u> underlines one of the themes of the play: <u>deception</u>.

Antonio enters under guard, and Cesario identifies him as the man who rescued 'him' from the duel. Orsino recognises him as a pirate who once attacked his fleet. Antonio complains of Cesario's ingratitude, of how Antonio rescued 'him' from the sea, risked arrest in order to accompany 'him', and even loaned 'him' his purse, only to be denied by 'that most ungrateful boy' when Antonio needed his help.

Cesario is as <u>confused</u> as the Duke by these allegations, and the Duke denies that they can be true, confirming that Cesario has been with him for the past three months. Further argument is prevented by Olivia's arrival.

Olivia again rejects Orsino's love and his response is angry, perhaps the first time he has spoken his mind. His vow to 'sacrifice' Cesario, whom he admits that he loves 'dearly', simply because he knows Olivia loves him, indicates the <u>turmoil in his own heart</u>. Viola now speaks out, declaring willingness to die 'a thousand deaths' for Orsino.

Olivia's clear rejection of Orsino <u>releases</u> Viola from her function as Orsino's agent. She can now <u>declare that she loves him</u> and is willing to follow him. This brings a horrified response from Olivia: 'Ay me, detested! How am I beguiled!' and she calls for the priest to back up her claim that she is Cesario's wife.

Viola's disguise now causes her to be blamed for everything. In the moments before the transformation, (s)he is spurned by the man she loves and the woman who thinks she loves her/him.

When the priest confirms he has married Cesario and Olivia, Viola is <u>trapped by her disguise</u>. The Duke calls her a 'dissembling cub', whilst Olivia begs her to tell the 'truth'. Then Sir Andrew enters and recounts how his head has been broken and Sir Toby given a 'bloody coxcomb too' during the duel with 'Cesario'. Sir Toby and Feste confirm Sir Andrew's story: Viola stands <u>accused on both sides</u>.

When Sebastian enters, Orsino sums up the vision before them, and encapsulates the amazement of all: 'One face, one voice, one habit, and two persons! / A natural perspective, that is and is not.' Sebastian, <u>unaware</u> for the moment of the <u>sensation he has created</u>, makes haste to apologise to Olivia for injuring her uncle, Sir Toby. He greets Antonio with great affection.

Explore

What do you think is
the dramatic effect of
Sebastian's entry here?

Brother and sister 'test' each other about their father and
childhood to make sure of each other's identity. Now
Viola can <u>tell the truth</u>, at last, about herself. Orsino says
that he too would like to share in this <u>amazing revelation</u>
of Cesario being a woman. He wants to see her in her
'woman's weeds'.

Interestingly, Viola stays in disguise until the end of the play
(the imprisoned Captain is the reason); equally interestingly,
she does not speak in reply to the Duke's proposal.

Feste delivers Malvolio's letter protesting his sanity, which
<u>convinces</u> Olivia that he is not mad. She asks for him to be
brought before her.

Happy at the way things have turned out, Orsino
<u>realises he is in love</u> with Viola, having grown to love
her while she was disguised as Cesario. He <u>proposes
marriage</u> to her and, given Viola's love for him, we may
assume she accepts.

Malvolio arrives and produces 'Olivia's' letter as evidence that
she has 'misused' him. Olivia recognises Maria's handwriting and
realises that <u>he has been hoaxed</u>. Fabian admits that what she
says is true, but pleads that it should not spoil the happiness
of the moment because, realising that his trick has put
Maria in a difficult position, Sir Toby has married her.

Feste <u>cannot resist goading</u> Malvolio, misquoting his
lines on greatness: 'and some have greatness thrown
upon them' and revealing that he was 'Sir Topas'. He
echoes Viola's belief that only time can sort matters out
when he says 'the whirligig of time brings in his
revenges'. But Malvolio <u>refuses to be placated</u>.
Outraged that he has been made to look foolish, he
leaves with threats to have revenge on everyone.

Explore

What effect is achieved
by first Feste and then
Fabian reading out
aloud Malvolio's letter?

Text commentary

59

"So comes it lady, you have been mistook"

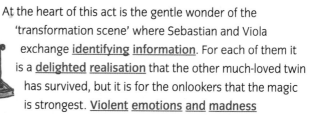

At the heart of this act is the gentle wonder of the 'transformation scene' where Sebastian and Viola exchange <u>identifying information</u>. For each of them it is a <u>delighted realisation</u> that the other much-loved twin has survived, but it is for the onlookers that the magic is strongest. <u>Violent emotions and madness disappear</u>, all are reconciled (if the attempt to 'entreat [Malvolio] to a peace' is successful) and reason prevails.

Finally, Orsino and Olivia agree: 'My lord, so please you... to think me as well a sister as a wife' / 'Madam, I am most apt t'embrace your offer.'

The last act assembles all the main players, except for the Captain, who was imprisoned on an unspecified charge made by Malvolio. Before the transformation every arrival seems to <u>increase confusion and madness</u>. After the transformation everything moves towards <u>reason and reconciliation</u>, partly because the existence of Sebastian explains so much, but for other reasons as well. The return of Feste brings a letter from Malvolio that, despite his reading, is self-evidently not the work of a madman. The <u>love stories are happily and suitably concluded</u>.

Feste's song ends the play and underlines the make-believe nature of it. It celebrates the traditional festive pursuits such as drinking and making merry. However, its repetition of 'For the rain it raineth every day' and repeated refernces to 'wind and rain' also contains a rather melancholy note which can be seen as muting to some extent the traditional happy ending. Think about Feste's final song. How can it be seen as a commentary on the play? Pick out references from the song to support your ideas.

Uncover the plot

Delete two of the three alternatives given, to find the correct plot.

1   *Orsino/Viola/the Captain finally arrives at Olivia's house, in time to back up Viola/Malvolio/Sir Toby against the accusations of Sebastian/Olivia/Antonio.*

2   *Olivia rejects Cesario's/Sebastian's/the Duke's love: enraged, he threatens Olivia/Cesario/Malvolio, but it is too late.*

3   *The Captain/Sebastian/Valentine turns up and all becomes clear. Viola, united with the Duke/Antonio/the Captain, asks for Malvolio/Antonio/the Captain to be set free.*

4   *Olivia, married to Cesario/Sebastian/Orsino, will be Viola's lover/subject/sister. A letter from Fabian/Sir Toby/Malvolio gains his release.*

Who? What? Why? Where? How?

1   *Who is Antonio, depending on the point of view of three other characters?*

2   *What does Antonio say he has given Sebastian?*

3   *Why has Sir Toby married Maria, according to Fabian?*

4   *Why does Fabian ask for leniency?*

5   *Where does Cesario go, when he is asked this question by Olivia?*

6   *How do Viola and Sebastian realise that they are brother and sister?*

Who said that?

1   *Who says: 'And I, most jocund, apt, and willingly/To do you rest, an thousand deaths would die'?*

2   *Who says: 'Be that thou know'st thou art', why, and why is this ironic?*

3   *Who says: 'How have the hours rack'd and tortur'd me/Since I have lost thee'?*

4   *Who says: 'If this be so, as yet the glass seems true/I shall have share in this most happy wreck'?*

5   *Who says: 'I'll be reveng'd on the whole pack of you'?*

- To prepare for an exam, you should read the text through at least twice, preferably three times. In order to answer an exam question on it you need to know it very well.

- When studyingly a play, such as *Twelfth Night*, you should try to see a performance of it. If you cannot see a live performance on stage, you should watch it on video or CD. You should be able to get a copy through your local library.

- If you are studying the text for an 'open book' exam, make sure that you take your copy of the text with you. However, do not rely on it too much – you haven't got time. If you are not allowed to take the text in with you, you will need to memorise brief quotations.

- Read all the questions carefully before deciding which one you are going to answer. Choose the question that best allows you to demonstrate your understanding and personal ideas.

- Make sure that you understand exactly what the question is asking you to do.

- Plan your answer carefully before starting to write your essay (see page 68).

- Always begin your answer with a short introduction which gives an overview of the topic. Use your plan to help keep you focused on the question as you write the essay. Try to leave enough time to write a brief conclusion.

- Remember to use the **point–quotation–comment** approach, where you make a point, support it with a short quotation, then comment on it. Use short and relevant quotations – do not waste time copying out chunks of the text.

- Make sure that you know how much time you have for each question and stick to it.

- Leave enough time at the end of the exam to check your work through carefully and correct any spelling or other mistakes that you have made.

- Timing is not as crucial for coursework essays, so this is your chance to show what you can really do, without having to write under pressure. Do not leave your coursework essays until the last minute though. If you have to rush your work it is unlikely to be the best you can produce.

- Coursework allows you to go into more detail and develop your ideas in greater depth. The required length of assignments varies, and your teacher will advise you on this.

- If you have a choice of title, make sure you choose one which you are interested in and which gives you the chance to develop your ideas.

- Plan your essay carefully (see page 68). Refer to your plan and the essay title as you write, to check that you are staying on course.

- Use quotations in your essay, but beware of using them too frequently or making them too long. Often, the best quotes are just one or two words or short phrases. Make sure that they are relevant to the points that you are making.

- If your topic requires it, use appropriate background information and put the text in a cultural and historical context. Remember, though, that the text itself should be at the centre of your essay.

- Include a short conclusion which sums up the key points of your ideas.

- Do not copy any of your essay from another source, e.g. other notes or the Internet. This is called plagiarism, and it is very serious if the exam board find that you have done this.

- If you have used sources, list them in a bibliography at the end of the essay.

- If you are allowed to word process your essay, it will be easier to make changes and to re-draft it.

Writing essays

Key quotations

> *If music be the food of love, play on,*
> *Give me excess of it; that surfeiting,*
> *The appetite may sicken, and so die.* (Act 1 Sc 1)

These lines are spoken by Orsino at the opening of the play. He is desperately in love with Olivia and the music feeds his passion for her. The quotation can be used to show the sentimental and affected nature of his love, which is later shown to have been an infatuation rather than genuine love.

> Cesario
> *Thou know'st no less but all. I have unclasped*
> *To thee the book even of my secret soul.* (Act 1 Sc 4)

These lines are spoken by Orsino to Viola/Cesario, and in them he refers to his love for Olivia. The quotation can be used to show how Cesario has quickly gained Orsino's trust to the point where he tells her his innermost secrets.

> O, you are sick of self-love, Malvolio and taste with a distempered appetite. (Act 1 Sc 5)

These lines are spoken by Olivia to Malvolio and in them she rebukes Malvolio for his selfish and self-centred behaviour. The quotation can be used to show how another character views Malvolio.

> *My masters, are you mad? Or what are you?*
> *Have you no wit, manners, nor honesty, but to gabble*
> *like tinkers at this time of night?* (Act 2 Sc 3)

These lines are spoken by Malvolio to Sir Toby and the others. Here he tells the others off, even though Sir Toby and Sir Andrew are his social superiors. The quotation can be used to show how Malvolio holds himself in high regard and feels that he has the moral superiority to chastise those who are of higher rank.

> *By maidhood, honour, truth and everything,*
> *I love thee so that, maugre all thy pride,*
> *Nor wit nor reason can my passion hide.* (Act 3 Sc 1)

These lines are spoken by Olivia to Viola/Cesario and in them Olivia openly states her love. The quotation can be used to show how what Olivia sees as a statement of her love is seen by the audience as evidence of the illusion on which her love is based.

> *Be not amazed. Right noble is his blood.*
> *If this be so, as yet the glass seems true,*
> *I shall have a share in this most happy wreck.*
> (Act 5 Sc 1)

These lines are spoken by Orsino to the gathered company in the final scene of the play. The quotation can be used to show how Orsino begins to view Cesario/Viola in a new light as the mistakes and illusions of the plot begin to be unravelled.

1. 'If music be the food of love, play on'. *In what ways are 'love' and 'music' important in the play?*

2. *Read again the passage near the end of the play (Act 5 Sc 1), from where Fabian enters with Malvolio, beginning:* DUKE: Is this the madman? *and ending:* OLIVIA: He has been most notoriously abused.

   Do you feel any sympathy for Malvolio here, and in the play as a whole?

3. *'The play begins in chaos and gradually moves towards harmony.' How true do you find this description of the plot of* Twelfth Night?

4. *By close reference to two or three scenes of the play, show how mistaken identity adds to the humour and excitement of the play.*

5. *Examine the role and importance of Feste in* Twelfth Night.

6. *Compare and contrast the attitudes towards love shown by Viola, Orsino and Olivia.*

7. *Examine the importance of the following characters in* Twelfth Night: *Maria; Sir Andrew; Fabian.*

8. *Viola has frequently been described as one of Shakespeare's most attractive characters. What attractive qualities do you find in her character?*

9. *What effects does Shakespeare achieve by alternating between poetry and prose? Refer to two scenes from the play to illustrate your comments.*

10 *Compare Shakepeare's presentation of the characters of Olivia and Orsino. Do you think the pair would have been well-matched?*

11 *How is the idea of order and disorder important to the play?*

12 *Olivia describes Malvolio as being 'sick of self-love'. Do you find this an accurate description of Malvolio?*

13 *What is the importance of music in* Twelfth Night?

14 *Discuss how Shakespeare produces comic elements in the play.*

15 *Discuss the character of Sir Toby Belch and his importance in* Twelfth Night.

16 *Compare the characters of Viola and Sebastian and the ways in which they are important in terms of the action of the play.*

17 *What role does disguise play in* Twelfth Night?

18 *Examine the ways in which the ideas of illusion and reality are important in the play.*

Planning an essay

In order to write an effective essay, you need to approach your task in an organised way. You need to **plan** your essay carefully before beginning to write. This will help you to achieve a higher grade.

● The first thing to do is read the question carefully to make sure that you fully understand it, then highlight key words.

● You will need to make notes on the topic in order to start preparing your ideas. You can do this in various ways, such as making a list of key points, or creating a spidergram or a mind map.

● One advantage of using mind maps or spidergrams is that they help you to create links between the various points you make. Put the title of the essay in the middle of a page and add your points around it. You can then draw lines to connect up various points or ideas, linking them in a clear, visual way.

● If you wish, you can colour code your ideas, or even add pictures or symbols if that helps you to think about your ideas more clearly.

● Since mind maps and spidergrams are a way of charting your knowledge, they are also an excellent revision aid. You could work through a number of essay titles in this way. (See some examples of spidergrams on the following pages.)

● In the planning stage of your essay it is also a good idea to jot down some useful quotations. These should be kept brief and to the point, and can be added to your spidergram.

● It can also be useful to plan what you are going to write in each paragraph of your essay. You can number the branches on your spidergram, so that you are clear about the order of your points. This will help you to structure your work more effectively.

● Remember that you are much more likely to write an effective essay if you do some planning before you start to write it.

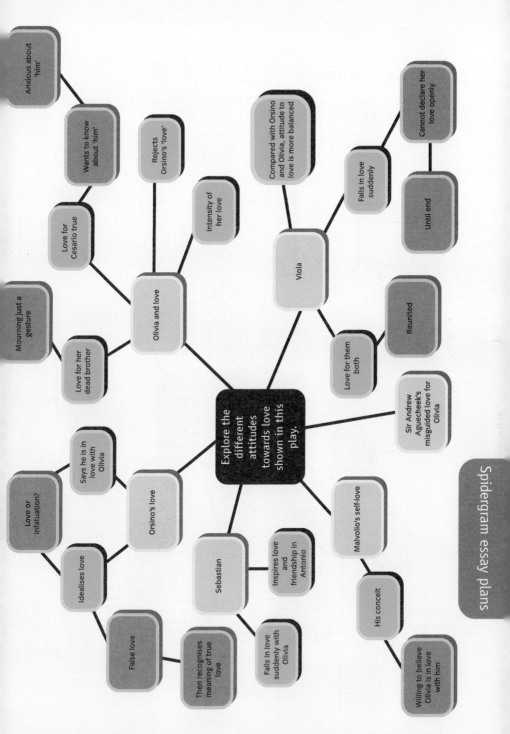

Explore the different attitudes towards love shown in this play.

Olivia and love
- Rejects Orsino's 'love'
- Intensity of her love
- Love for Cesario true
  - Anxious about 'him'
  - Wants to know about 'him'
- Love for her dead brother
  - Mourning just a gesture

Viola
- Compared with Orsino and Olivia, attitude to love is more balanced
- Falls in love suddenly
  - Cannot declare her love openly
  - Until end
- Love for them both
  - Reunited

Sir Andrew Aguecheek's misguided love for Olivia

Orsino's love
- Says he is in love with Olivia
  - Love or infatuation?
- Idealises love
  - False love

Sebastian
- Inspires love and friendship in Antonio
- Then recognises meaning of true love
- Falls in love suddenly with Olivia

Malvolio's self-love
- His conceit
  - Willing to believe Olivia is in love with him

Spidergram essay plans

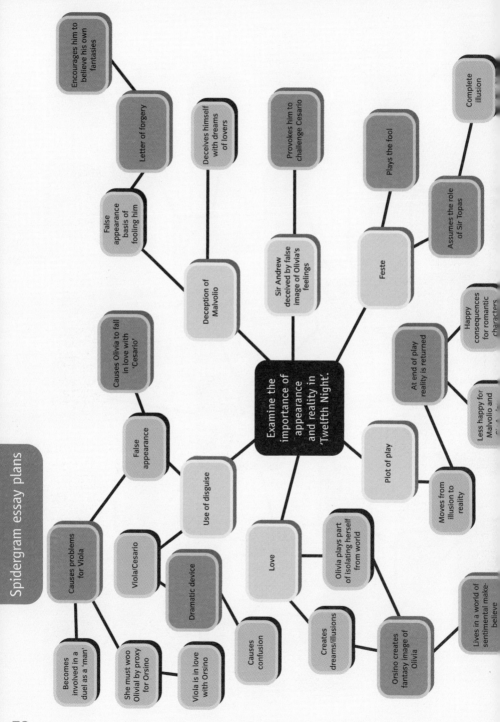

Examine the importance of appearance and reality in 'Twelfth Night'.

Deception of Malvolio
- False appearance basis of fooling him
  - Letter of forgery
    - Encourages him to believe his own fantasies
- Deceives himself with dreams of lovers

Sir Andrew deceived by false image of Olivia's feelings
- Provokes him to challenge Cesario

Feste
- Plays the fool
- Assumes the role of Sir Topas
  - Complete illusion

Use of disguise
- False appearance
  - Causes Olivia to fall in love with 'Cesario'
  - Viola/Cesario
    - Causes problems for Viola
      - Becomes involved in a duel as a 'man'
      - She must woo Olivia by proxy for Orsino
      - Viola is in love with Orsino
- Dramatic device
  - Causes confusion
  - Creates dreams/illusions

Love
- Olivia plays part of isolating herself from world
- Orsino creates fantasy image of Olivia
  - Lives in a world of sentimental make-believe

Plot of play
- Moves from illusion to reality
- At end of play reality is returned
  - Happy consequences for romantic characters
  - Less happy for Malvolio and

Spidergram essay plans

How is the idea of order and disorder important in the play?

Disorder

- **Lord of 'Misrule'**
  - Tradition of 'Festive Season'
    - Relaxation of order
  - Confusion
    - Disguises
      - Lack of understanding
- **Feste**
- **Sir Toby**
  - Wild behaviour
    - Rebuked by Maria
    - Rebuked by Malvolio
    - Continued by Olivia!
  - Sir Andrew
  - A threat to harmony
    - Breach of order
- **Challenge to authority**
  - Puritanism of Malvolio

Order

- **Viola breaches 'order' by disguise**
  - Order restored when identity revealed
    - Sebastian and Viola restored to orderly world
- **Ending of play**
- **Attempts to establish order**
  - 'Malvolio' reflects disorder
- **Order returned at end**
  - Malvolio not content
- **Harmony of ending**
  - Sebastian/Olivia
  - Viola/Orsino
  - Sir Toby/Maria

71

Sample response

Discuss the presentations of Viola and Sebastian. What is their importance as characters within the play?

We first see Viola in Act 1 Sc 2, when she has survived a shipwreck, but she is afraid her twin brother, Sebastian, hasn't.✓ Here she is seen to be a caring sister as she worries about the safety of her brother: "O, my poor brother!" ✓ However, the Captain who has seen her to safety reassures her that he has seen Sebastian alive since the ship broke upon the rocks. Also in this scene Viola is presented as being curious and resourceful.✓ She asks many questions of the Captain as she tries to get some information on the strange place Illyria.✓

We can see her resourcefulness as she tries to get a plan of how she can get by in Illyria. She first thinks that she might be able to serve Olivia: "O that I served that lady, And might not be delivered to the world/Till I had made mine own occasion mellow, What my estate is!" ✓ However, the Captain explains to her that this would be practically impossible as Olivia "will admit no kind of suit". Through her response to this we can see that Viola is trusting and willing to take advice. ✓

She shows her confidence ✓ as she then decides to dress as a boy with the Captain's help and go and work for the Duke. She outlines qualities that she has which will help her to secure a job with him: "I can sing and speak to him in many sorts of music". This shows that she is a confident young woman who is resourceful and determined. ✓

Dressed as a young man, Viola, now Cesario, is presented as being successful as she not only secures a job working for the Duke but she has become one of his favourite workers after only a short time. ✓ As Valentine says to Cesario: 'If the Duke continue these favours towards you/Cesario, you are like to be much advanced; he hath/known you but three days and already you are no stranger'.

Cesario also succeeds in winning Orsino's trust as he confides in her about his love for Olivia, so we get the impression that Viola is presented as a good, patient listener. ✓

Through the character Viola, because she takes on the role of a young man, Shakespeare adds to the humour of the play as a whole. ✓ Not only through Cesario wooing Olivia on Orsino's behalf, only to find out that Olivia likes her instead, but also because Viola herself falls in love with Orsino. ✓ The confusion that this disguise creates in the play is important to the play, not only for humour but because the confusion created makes a successful conclusion possible as everything comes out into the open and is resolved. ✓ Sebastian has very similar character traits to Viola, which is not surprising seeing as he is her identical twin. He has a smaller role in the play, but is important because he is mistaken for Viola and this all adds to the confusion and comedy of the play.

Examiner's comments

This is a sound response in which the student shows a clear understanding of the characters. Some insight and evaluation is evident and textual references used. However, the quotations could be used to develop discussion further. The points that are made have been carefully selected and are accompanied by accurate supporting detail, and there is some exploration of ideas. Viola is dealt with in some detail, although there could have been a greater focus on the character of Sebastian.

Sample response

> **Discuss the presentations of Viola and Sebastian. What is their importance as characters within the play?**
>
> Viola and Sebastian are identical twins and, in many ways, they exhibit very similar characteristics too. ✓ Viola is presented as the classic, romantic heroine and, because she spends most of the play disguised as a man, she is shown responding to a wider variety of situations. ✓
>
> One of the key points about Viola's character is the liveliness and wit that she shows, and it is this aspect of her character that Olivia finds attractive. After meeting her for the first time (as Cesario) Olivia immediately detects a nobility ✓ in Viola's character: 'Thy tongue, thy face, thy limbs, actions and spirits,/Do give thee five-fold blazon', ✓ and she clearly is attracted to her: 'Even so quickly may one catch the plague?/Methinks I feel this youth's perfections/With an invisible and subtle stealth/To creep in at mine eyes.' ✓
>
> Even through her disguise Orsino senses her femininity, ✓ even though he is completely convinced that Cesario is a boy: 'For they shall yet belie thy happy years/That say thou art a man; Diana's lip/Is not more smooth and rubious; thy small pipe/Is as the maiden's organ, shrill and sound,/And all is semblative a woman's part.' ✓
>
> Although her disguise convinces everyone, even Viola finds it difficult to cope with the prospect of fighting a duel, ✓ although once again she shows her ability to think and act quickly to deal with the situation. ✓

Overall, Viola's disguise, though, is more than a dramatic device; it also allows her to display the full range of her character.✓

Just as Viola is presented as the classic romantic heroine, her twin, Sebastian, can be seen as the traditional romantic hero – handsome, generous, noble and brave.✓ Sebastian, like Viola, inspires loyalty and affection in others, as can be seen by the way Antonio holds him in high regard. Olivia responds to Sebastian in just the same way✓ as she responds to Viola/Cesario, understandably because she thinks he actually is Cesario.✓

Like Viola, who shows loyalty to Orsino, Sebastian shows loyalty ✓ to Antonio, and to Olivia when he makes a commitment to her. He detects her qualities immediately, without which: 'She could not sway her house, command her followers,/Take and give back affairs and their dispatch/With such a smooth, discreet, and stable bearing/As I perceive she does.' ✓

Some critics have said that he shows opportunist characteristics because of the speed and readiness with which he accepts Olivia's proposal but, of course, this is a dramatic necessity ✓ for the working out of the plot.

Sebastian also adds to the confusion when he turns up in Illyria.✓ He is presented as more of a minor character, ✓ as he only comes in to the play near the end. His physical presentation must mean that he looks very like Viola as they both manage to fool most of the other characters. ✓ However, his character is not as detailed ✓ as that of Viola and we see him falling in love with Olivia very quickly without knowing anything about her because he hasn't had much chance to get to know her. Whereas Viola's love for Orsino seems more sincere because she has had time to get to know and fall in love with him, which shows her to be more level-headed.

In conclusion, Viola and Sebastian, although very alike to look at, ✓ are very different natured and are presented differently. They both provide humour through the confusion their characters create, ✓ which also allows a successful conclusion when their true identities are revealed and a happy double wedding provides a neat conclusion to the play.

Examiner's comments

This is a very good response, which shows a detailed understanding of the characters and shows a sense of critical response to the task. There is much clear and perceptive evaluation of the ways in which the characters are presented, together with some well-supported personal views. The textual support is appropriate and well-chosen and is used effectively to illustrate various points. There is much detail in the analysis of Viola, but there is also a good focus on Sebastian. A clear awareness is shown of the dramatic functions of these characters in the drama.

Quick quiz answers

Quick quiz 1

Uncover the plot

1   Illyria; the Duke Orsino; Olivia; brother
2   Viola; Cesario
3   three; to woo Olivia
4   Orsino
5   Maria; Sir Andrew Aguecheek

What? Why? How? Where? When?

1   to be 'generous, guiltless and of free disposition' (1, 5)
2   'Better a witty fool than a foolish wit' (1, 5)
3   because the show of passion will be more appealing in a younger 'man' (1, 5)
4   'With adorations, fertile tears, with groans that thunder love, with sighs of fire.' (1, 5)
5   in Elysium; he is dead (in paradise) (1, 2)
6   the following day; another month; because Sir Toby is living off his money (1, 3)

Who said that?

1   Orsino (1, 1)
2   Viola (1, 2)
3   Sir Toby Belch (1, 3)
4   Malvolio (1, 5)
5   Olivia (1, 5)

Quick quiz 2

Uncover the plot

1   Olivia; Orsino; Olivia
2   Feste; stronger
3   Malvolio; singing
4   Maria; handwriting; marry him
5   Sir Andrew

Who? What? Why? How?

1   Malvolio (2, 3)
2   the melody Viola and the Duke are listening to (2, 4)
3   lovers meeting (2, 3)
4   Maria has told him so; she treats him with respect; the letter forged by Maria (2, 5)
5   because it was old-fashioned, plain and innocent – not like the more modern songs (2, 4)
6   in the sunlight, talking to his shadow (2, 5)

Who said that?

1   Sebastian, of his sister (whom we suspect to be Viola) (2, 1)
2   Antonio (2, 1)
3   Malvolio (2, 3)
4   Orsino; because Viola is suffering the pangs of love for Orsino (2, 4)

Quick quiz 3

Uncover the plot
1. press the Duke's suit
2. Cesario
3. Sir Andrew's; devil
4. Antonio; purse; Viola
5. Sebastian

Who? What? Why? How?
1. Malvolio, because he is just about to show himself anything but (3, 4)
2. refusing to return what was taken in the sea fight against the Duke's galleys (3, 3)
3. the joke of Sir Andrew's challenge to Cesario: Malvolio's apparent madness before Olivia (3, 4)
4. in order to make Sir Andrew jealous (3, 2)
5. his help (with the duel) and his predicament – he thinks she is Sebastian, to whom he has lent it (3, 4)
6. that in fact it is he who has been 'dear' (expensive) to Sir Andrew, by getting money from him (3, 4)

Who said that?
1. Olivia (3, 1)
2. Antonio (3, 3)
3. Viola (3, 4)
4. Olivia (3, 4)
5. Malvolio (3, 4)

Quick quiz 4

Uncover the plot
1. Cesario; Sebastian
2. Sir Andrew; hits back
3. Olivia; Cesario; Sir Toby
4. Feste; Sir Topas; afraid
5. Olivia; marry her

Who? What? Why? How?
1. Sir Toby (4, 1)
2. Antonio; he thinks he has just missed him – he is actually under arrest (4, 3)
3. a pearl; she has already sent Cesario a ring and given him a jewel/portrait (4, 3)
4. because it is dangerous; he is already in trouble with Olivia (4, 2)
5. Sir Andrew expects the 'cowardly' Cesario; Sebastian knows nothing of the previous quarrel (4, 1)
6. with a 'smooth, discreet and stable bearing' (4, 3)

Who said that?
1. Malvolio (4, 2)
2. Sir Topas (Feste) to Malvolio (4, 2)
3. Sebastian (4, 3)
4. Olivia – it seems hasty to her, and she has 'courted' Cesario; as far as Sebastian is concerned, they have only just met (4, 3)
5. Sir toby (4, 2)

Quick quiz 5

Uncover the plot

1 Orsino; Viola; Antonio
2 the Duke's love; Cesario
3 Sebastian; the Duke; the Captain
4 Sebastian; sister; Malvolio.

Who? What? Why? Where? How?

1 to Viola, the man who rescued her from the duel; to Orsino, a 'notable pirate'; to Sebastian, a dear re-found friend (5, 1)
2 Sebastian's life, and also his love 'without retention or restraint' (5, 1)
3 in 'recompense' for writing the letter which ensnared Malvolio (5, 1)
4 first, not to mar the happiness of the time; second, because there is a fault on both sides (5, 1)
5 to follow his master, the Duke, who is leaving in a rage – even if the Duke will kill him (5, 1)
6 They refer to a brother/sister of the same name. Their father(s) have the same name, 'both' have a mole on the brow and 'both' died when Viola was 13 years old (5, 1)

Who said that?

1 Viola/Cesario (5, 1)
2 Olivia; to urge Cesario to be bold (he 'is' her husband). In fact, what he 'is', nobody yet knows! (5, 1)
3 Antonio (5, 1)
4 Duke Orsino (5, 1)
5 Malvolio (5, 1)

First published 1994
Revised edition 2004

Letts Educational
Chiswick Centre
414 Chiswick High Road
London W4 5TF
Tel: 020 8996 3333

Cover and text design by Hardlines Ltd., Charlbury, Oxfordshire.

Typeset by Letterpart Ltd., Reigate, Surrey.

Graphic illustration by Beehive Illustration, Cirencester, Gloucestershire.

Commissioned by Cassandra Birmingham

Editorial project management by Jo Kemp

Printed in Italy.

British Library Cataloguing in Publication Data. A CIP record of this book is
available from the British Library.

ISBN 1 84315 332 8

Letts Educational is a division of Granada Learning, part of Granada plc.